CHAMPNEYS COOKBOOK

Adam Palmer

CHAMPNEYS
COOKBOOK

Adam Palmer

Ward Lock
London

First published in the United Kingdom in 1999 by Ward Lock

Text copyright © The Champneys Group Ltd, 1999
Design and layout copyright © Weidenfeld & Nicolson, 1999

The moral right of The Champneys Group Ltd to be identified as the author of this work
has been asserted in accordance with the Copyright, Designs and Patents Act 1988

A CIP catalogue record for this book is available from the British Library

ISBN 0297 82521 6

Art Directed by David Rowley
Photographs by Philip Webb
Designed by Lucy Holmes
Edited by Maggie Ramsay
Typeset by Tiger Typeset
Printed and bound in Italy

Ward Lock
Illustrated Division
The Orion Publishing Group
Wellington House
125 Strand
London WC2R 0BB

contents

part one

Philosophy
The Champneys health philosophy is based not on calorie counting, but on balance, moderation and variety.

part two

Recipes
More than 100 recipes for breakfast, lunch and dinner, including low fat versions of traditional desserts.

foreword

There are few cooks of whom it can be said 'he changed my life', but Adam Palmer is such a man. For many years he has devoted his immense talents to proving that gourmet food and healthy eating can not only be synonymous but that under the guiding principles of Champneys – moderation and balance – he can produce dishes to match the best London restaurants.

When I first came to Champneys, I was a pretty average fortysomething, unfit and overweight. Being in a career running some of the best hotels in the world, I reckoned I knew all there was to know about food.

My discovery of Champneys turned out to be full of surprises. My misconceptions tumbled one by one. The first delightful surprise was the stunning food Adam was producing. Like many, I thought healthy food was boring and tasteless, and to discover beautifully presented dishes full of flavour and texture shattered that misconception. As a foodie I was fascinated and I have since spent many happy hours discussing food with Adam.

Adam combines two important skills: first and last he is a great chef with the instinctive flair for taste that all great chefs have, but equally as important he has an encyclopaedic knowledge of food properties and science, which enables him to create delicious dishes that just happen to be healthy. The resulting combination of science and art has produced a repertoire of outstanding dishes, each a masterpiece of taste and texture in its own right but each also carefully crafted to help form part of a balanced and healthy diet.

For me, meeting Adam has been a godsend. Between the kitchen and the gym I have lost 3½ stone and managed to keep most of it off – the result is I feel great. But most important of all I have discovered through Adam that with a little knowledge and planning the best things in life are not only good for you but also delicious.

Thinking of Adam's food reminds me of the 1960s' beer advert: 'Looks good, tastes good and by golly it does you good'. I hope you enjoy cooking it as much as I enjoy eating it.

The Viscount Thurso
Managing Director

introduction

Healthy eating is all about balance and I do not believe that any one ingredient is bad for you. However, far too many people eat too much of certain foods and not enough of others. The food I have created at Champneys and in this book goes some way towards correcting the balance.

It is very difficult to maintain a healthy, balanced diet if the only consideration is how many calories you are consuming every day. It is far better to think about food as part of the wider picture of your lifestyle, rather than just 'going for the big burn' on calories. It is important to keep yourself motivated, and this means eating the foods that you enjoy, using the fantastic array of flavours, cooking styles and influences from various countries.

Fat is one thing we consume to excess, particularly animal fats such as butter and cream. Cream and butter can give thickness, body and a silky finish to sauces; but in my opinion they are often overused by chefs. So I do not use them – although it is very tempting sometimes! However, if you are not finishing a dish with cream or butter you must compensate by using other flavours during cooking.

Salt, again, we all eat too much of. Processed foods, such as breakfast cereals, often contain surprisingly high amounts of salt. While we should be cautious when using salt, remember that seasoning is important; if you do not season food correctly, all the hard work that goes into creating a tantalizing meal will be wasted. Season food after tasting it, and use salt to enhance the flavour of the food, not overwhelm it. You can reduce the need for salt by using strong, robust flavours in your cooking: the zest and juice of lemons and limes, spices and fresh herbs.

If you consume too much sugar you will probably put on excess weight. But sugar is a natural food and I prefer to use it in moderation rather than its nasty-tasting alternatives, many of which now carry a health warning.

Enough of the bad guys. There are two key areas where we should be looking to increase our intake of certain foods. The first is fibre. Fibre sounds like hard work – brown, dry and tasteless – but this is not the whole story. There are plenty of exciting ingredients that contain fibre, such as couscous, rice and polenta, while fresh fruit and vegetables – excellent fibre-providers – are a mainstay of Champneys' cuisine.

Since I began looking into organic and naturally produced foods, I have become convinced that we should all be demanding that food producers stop the madness of artificially produced, chemically enhanced and intensively grown food. Is it too much to ask that our foods are produced naturally? Organic foods are, unfortunately, often expensive, but cheap food is not always good food. It is very likely to be full of additives and pesticide residues, which are surely detrimental to health. If we accept short cuts in food production we must also accept that there may be a price to pay in the long term. Who knows, maybe some day we will return to buying food in season when it is at its best – in nutritional value, price, quality and taste.

Far too many people fail to accept that healthy eating could fit into their lifestyle on a daily basis; they still think that healthy food means brown, vegetarian or just downright cranky. It isn't and does not have to be – wake up, smell the coffee.

Adam Palmer
Executive Chef

useful equipment

non-stick frying pan with metal handle
Invaluable for cooking without adding fat. I usually heat it before adding the food; the food is then quickly sealed or browned, and the pan can be put into the oven to finish cooking. An enamelled cast-iron pan (such as those made by Le Creuset) could be used in the same way.

stainless steel saucepans
Good quality, thick-bottomed pans help cook food evenly, without sticking or burning.

casserole dish
Ideally, this will be flameproof so it can be used on top of the stove or in the oven. It should have a tight-fitting lid to seal in the steam and keep food moist and tender.

griddle pan
Non-stick is best, but even uncoated pans are great for cooking food quickly, with a minimum of fat, leaving distinctive blackened 'grill lines'.

non-stick pancake pan
Not essential, but a 20 cm/8 inch diameter non-stick frying pan allows you to make savoury or sweet pancakes with a minimum of fat.

non-stick roasting tin
Choose a good quality tin that can be placed on top of the stove without buckling.

baking sheet
Again, choose a thick, good quality baking sheet for versatility.

wok
The shape of a wok is ideal for stir-frying, a healthy cooking method. I use a wok with a tight-fitting lid for smoking fish – a quick and easy way to discover a new flavour.

bamboo steamer
Use to cook vegetables or reheat delicate items.

terrine or loaf tin
I use a terrine to prepare both sweet and savoury dishes – a loaf tin would do just as well. A 1 litre/1¾ pint terrine is perfect for serving 8–10 people.

gateau ring
A set of four or six individual (7 cm/2¾ inch diameter, 4 cm/1½ inch deep) gateau rings is useful for making chilled desserts.
Alternatively, use ramekins; sometimes you will need to line the base with a circle of baking parchment.

pastry cutters
A set of pastry cutters in various sizes can be used for pastry, biscuits, rosti and evenly shaped fish cakes.

hand-held blender
Perfect for liquidizing soups and sauces in the pan in which they are cooked.

pestle and mortar
Useful for blending herb and spice mixtures where there is little or no liquid. Choose a heavy pestle, which will make grinding easier.

grater
A hand-held grater is fine, but a food processor makes it easy to grate large quantities.

mandolin slicer
Not essential, but useful for cutting uniformly thin slices of vegetables.

baking parchment
Rather than oiling a baking sheet, line it with baking parchment (non-stick baking paper).

cooking oil in a spray can or pump
Sometimes you need to use a little oil to prevent ingredients from sticking; vegetable oils such as sunflower and olive are now available in spray cans. The fine mist allows you to use the minimum amount of oil.

philosophy

1

healthy eating, the champneys way

Champneys' approach to healthy eating is based on our belief in variety, moderation and balance. It is a simple but sophisticated philosophy that takes into account not only recent international research in the field of nutrition and dietetics but also the changing needs of individuals.

Our policy on food and nutrition steers away from myths and misconceptions and keeps healthy eating simple and enjoyable. Calorie counting is no longer a regime imposed on Champneys' guests. Instead, we keep a careful check on calories through methods of preparation and cooking techniques and by controlling the size of portions. Menus are planned to maximize healthy choices throughout the day and all meals are based on current dietary guidelines for optimum nutritional health.

Champneys follows three key principles for healthy eating:

Moderation
This is defined both by portion size and also by how often a particular food is consumed. Foods are not classified as 'good' or 'bad', but no food, or type of food, should be eaten to excess.

Balance
Healthy eating habits include foods from each of the main food groups: starchy foods and cereal grains; fruit and vegetables; meat, poultry and fish or protein alternatives; dairy foods.

Variety
Variety, the spice of life, is a health essential: to obtain the necessary vitamins, minerals and other nutrients, the body needs a wide range of foods from the different food groups.

We also have a policy of obtaining products fom organic or naturally farmed sources wherever possible. We believe such foods not only taste better but are also far less likely to have detrimental effects on health in the long term.

The Champneys way focuses on eating less fat and more fibre, rather than counting calories. For most people, a healthy diet is:

• high in fibre, obtained from an adequate intake of vegetables, , beans and pulses, fruits and complex carbohydrates such as cereals and grains.

• low in fat, especially saturated fats (those of animal origin and hard at room temperature). Polyunsaturated and monounsaturated fats and fish oils are beneficial in small quantities.

Protein intake should be moderate, and in balance with other foods.

At Champneys we offer a variety of tempting choices at breakfast, lunch and dinner. The nutritive value of all foods is calculated using specialized computer software, assessed according to fat and fibre content and coded with symbols alongside each dish.

Hearts indicate fat content: saturated fat is illustrated by a solid heart, unsaturated fat by a heart in a circle. Fibre is indicated by one, two or three apples; the greater the number of apples the higher the fibre content. Codings are per serving.

♥ Very low fat (5 g or less)

♥♥ Low fat (5–10 g)

♥♥♥ Medium fat (10–20 g)

♥ Unsaturated fats-*this symbol appears on recipes containing unsaturated fats: it is not an indication of additional fat and the total fat content might still be very low.*

🍎 Low fibre (2 g or less)

🍎🍎 Medium fibre (2–5 g)

🍎🍎🍎 High fibre (over 5 g)

what your body needs

Healthy eating messages appear everywhere: in books and magazines, on television and food packaging, and in government guidelines based on scientific research. Yet many people, although familiar with the idea of eating less fat and more fibre, lack a clear understanding of the make-up of a healthy diet and are therefore unable to make well-informed choices in changing their eating habits and lifestyle. For example, filling a shopping trolley with fat-free or low-fat products does not guarantee freedom from ill health, unless the rest of the diet is balanced. (The diet consists of those foods or mixtures of foods in the amounts which are actually eaten.) A good diet will provide adequate amounts of all nutrients, without harmful excesses, from a wide range of foods.

My objective is to shed some light on how a balanced diet can be achieved – whether for weight loss or for the maintenance of health and a wonderful feeling of vitality.

Foods provide energy and nourishment for survival and enjoyment of life. Too little food – or too much – can lead to ill health. Many common health problems, such as obesity, heart disease, diabetes, arthritis and various forms of cancer, are linked to diet either directly or indirectly.

While people are busy achieving life goals and developing their careers, the processes of narrowing and hardening of the arteries might be silently taking place within their bodies, especially if they eat a lot of cheese, butter, cream and fatty meat or high-fat snacks such as chocolate, biscuits and crisps. Overweight adults are at risk of developing adult-onset diabetes. Nutritionally related illnesses often take a long time to come to light, and when diagnosed they may demand severe restrictions of the diet. Many health problems that afflict middle-aged and older people could have been avoided had some time been invested in assessing and maintaining nutritional health earlier in life.

Food energy

The body needs energy to function and survive. Food provides the energy which is used for bodily processes (such as breathing, body temperature maintenance, digestion, absorption and metabolism of food) and physical activities (such as walking, running, swimming, gardening). However, when food is eaten in excess of the body's energy requirements, it will be converted into body fat. Obesity brings its own potential problems, such as high blood pressure and coronary heart disease.

Energy is measured in kilo-calories (kcal) or kilo-Joules (kJ) in the same way that weight is measured in stones and pounds or kilograms. For simplicity, energy is generally referred to as calories, although nutritionists express it as kcal.

The energy provided by carbohydrate, fat, protein and other constituents can be measured and used to calculate the energy value (calorific value) of any food, diet or recipe.

• 1g (gram) of dietary carbohydrate provides 3.75–4 kcal of energy. There are three main categories of carbohydrates: sugar and starch, which are major sources of energy, and non–starch polysaccharides (NSP), collectively known as fibre. Fibre, which does not provide energy so is not strictly speaking a nutrient, has important positive effects on health.

Carbohydrates may be converted into body fat if taken in excess; for some people, sweets, desserts and fizzy drinks represent significant sources of energy.

• 1g of dietary fat provides 9 kcal. There are two main types of fats: saturated and unsaturated (monounsaturated and polyunsaturated). They include both fats and oils and provide more than twice as many calories per gram as carbohydrates. Food fats can easily be converted into body fat if taken in excess.

• 1g of dietary protein provides 4 kcal. Protein provides the body with amino acids that are essential for growth and repair. It can also be converted within the body into carbohydrate to provide energy.

• 1g of dietary alcohol provides 7 kcal. It is considered as a food because it provides energy, even though it has drug-like properties and no other nutritive value.

Water, vitamins, minerals and fibre do not provide energy. Almost all foods are composed of water, carbohydrates, proteins and fat in varying degrees. Foods that contain a large amount of water such as vegetables, fruits and clear soups usually contain little protein, fat, or carbohydrate and hence few calories.

Knowledge of the above values can help in identifying sources of calories in the diet. For instance, one might be eating a healthy, well-balanced diet, but still experience some weight problems if alcohol intake isn't taken into account. Foods rich in fat such as cheese and oils are concentrated sources of energy, as are sugars. Reducing calories in order to achieve weight loss means reducing the consumption of energy-dense food (fat, sugar, alcohol) as well as portion sizes, a practical approach that works very well at Champneys.

Now let's look at the main food groups and their characteristics in more detail.

Carbohydrates

Although sugars and starch have similar amounts of calories, they are used by the body in different ways.

Sugars

Sugars provide readily available energy, and are found in a number of forms. Any of the following names may be seen on manufactured foods, including soft drinks, biscuits and jams, and also on savoury items such as soups and dressings. Remember that they are all sugars and should be consumed in moderation, especially if a reduction in energy intake is needed.

Glucose, also known as dextrose, occurs naturally in fruit. Fructose occurs naturally in some fruits and in honey; it is the sweetest sugar known. Sucrose (table sugar) occurs naturally in sugar cane and sugar beet, and in lesser quantities in fruits and some root vegetables such as carrots and sweet potatoes. Lactose (milk sugar) occurs only in milk; it is less sweet than sucrose or glucose. Maltose is formed in the body during the breakdown of starch by digestive enzymes and, for instance, when grains are germinated for the production of beer.

Starch

According to current healthy eating guidelines, complex carbohydrate or starchy foods should provide the major part of our food energy. An adequate intake of starchy foods also helps to sustain normal blood sugar level during exercise and hence conserve muscle mass, diminish hunger pangs and prevent symptoms of mild hypoglycaemia (dizziness, lack of concentration, fatigue). Such foods include potatoes, pasta, rice, cracked wheat, couscous, polenta, oats and other cereals and grains.

It is recommended that carbohydrate should contribute at least 50% of our total energy intake. This means that in a diet of 2000 kcal a day, 1000 kcal would come from carbohydrate (equivalent to about 250 g of carbohydrate). Ideally, 40% should come from starch and the types of sugars found in milk and whole fruits and vegetables, while the sugars from fruit juices, sucrose and sugars added to foods should contribute no more than 10% of dietary energy.

A recent UK study showed that, on average, sugars contributed 36% of total carbohydrate intake, with 7% of this figure coming from the lactose in dairy products. This is in contrast to what was the norm a century ago, when flour and potato consumption was much higher than that of sugars.

Fibre

In addition to starch, there are other carbohydrates found in the cell walls of fruits, vegetables, pulses and cereal grains. These compounds are classified as fibre.

The fibre in wheat (such as in wholemeal bread and wholegrain breakfast cereals), maize and rice is mainly insoluble cellulose and related materials. Insoluble fibre is not absorbed into the body, but adds bulk to the faeces and hence helps to prevent constipation. This property plays an important role in preventing many serious illnesses, including bowel cancer and disorders of the digestive system.

Fruits, vegetables, oats, barley, rye, beans and lentils contain soluble forms of fibre. Soluble fibre may be absorbed by the body and can help to reduce blood levels of low density lipoprotein (LDL) cholesterol (the undesirable cholesterol that can block the arteries) and increase high density lipoprotein cholesterol (HDL, the form of cholesterol that can 'cleanse' the arteries). Soluble fibre also plays a key role in regulating blood sugar levels.

Pectin – which is found in apples and many other fruits and in root vegetables such as turnips and sweet potatoes – is not fibrous, and because it is completely digested, it has little effect on the regulation of bowel movement. However, pectin has a similar effect to soluble fibre in helping to reduce blood LDL cholesterol levels and blood sugar concentration.

As the effects of both soluble and insoluble fibre are beneficial, a variety of fibre-rich foods should be eaten every day. The daily intake of fibre in the UK currently averages about 12g a day; an increase to 18g a day is recommended.

When a reduction in the fat content of the diet is desired, the best way of replacing some of the energy is by increasing the consumption of fibre-rich starchy foods such as wholegrain breakfast cereals, wholewheat pasta and cereal grains, including rice, oats and millet. This approach is at the heart of Champneys' philosophy on weight management.

Proteins

Proteins provide amino acids for growth and repair. The body can also convert them into glucose to be used for energy when there is a limited supply of carbohydrate. That is why restricting carbohydrate intake or following a high protein diet can be disadvantageous as this might force the body to use protein for energy production, which is not its prime physiological role. Balancing the diet in terms of protein and carbohydrates is important in weight-reducing diets in order to prevent the breakdown of muscle proteins which results in unsafe weight loss.

There are two groups of proteins - animal and vegetable proteins. Animal proteins, found in meat, fish, poultry and game, eggs, cheese and milk, have high biological value because they contain all the amino acids the human body requires. However, their main nutritional advantage over vegetable foods is that they contain nutrients such as vitamin B12, iron, zinc and vitamin A.

Plant proteins are found in pulses and nuts, and also in cereal grains, including wheat (pasta, couscous, cracked wheat), maize (corn), millet and rice, and potatoes. They are referred to as low biological value proteins because they are generally low or lacking in one or two of the essential amino acids. However, mixtures of plant protein foods complement each other, so that even among those who eat no animal proteins, protein deficiency is rarely a problem provided that they eat a wide variety of foods from the main food groups. Examples of vegetable protein combinations include beans on toast, a vegetable stir-fry with cashew nuts and noodles, spicy lentils served with rice, or breakfast cereal with cows' milk or soya milk.

There is a growing demand for sources of protein that can replace animal-based proteins in the diet. Besides tofu (bean curd), a traditional ingredient in far Eastern cuisine, other meat-free protein foods include textured vegetable protein (TVP) such as soya mince or soya chunks and mycoprotein (for example Quorn products). Some of these products are fortified with vitamins and minerals, such as iron, zinc and some of the B-vitamins.

Fat

Chemically there is little difference between fats and oils, but there are nonetheless different types of fat. Saturated fats are primarily of animal origin: butter and lard, fatty parts of meat and the skin of poultry and game. Cream, cheese and, surprisingly, coconut oil also contain high proportions of saturated fat. The problem with this type of fat is its link with LDL cholesterol, which can have serious effects on cardiovascular health. Replacing saturated fats in the diet with monounsaturated (olive oil, nut oils) or polyunsaturated fats (such as corn or sunflower oil) can help to lower LDL cholesterol levels.

Animal fats may contain vitamin A and vitamin D, vegetable fats may contain beta-carotene (a form of vitamin A) and vitamin E. All are equally high in calories. Healthy eating guidelines suggest that fats should provide 30–35% of our total energy, or 600 –700 kcal of a 2000 kcal a day intake; this represents a total of 67–78 g of fat a day.

In nutrition, a distinction is often made between 'visible' and 'invisible' fats. Visible fats are those clearly apparent to the consumer, including fat spreads, cooking oils and the fat around meat. In contrast, a great deal of the fat we consume is hidden during manufacturing and cooking, for instance in cakes and biscuits, in pâtés and sausages and in emulsions such as mayonnaise and dressings. Many foods also contain a proportion of 'invisible' fat; these include lean meat, fish, eggs, milk, cheeses and grains.

A reduction in total fat intake can therefore be achieved not only by cutting down on visible fats and adopting lower fat cooking methods, but also by becoming aware of hidden sources of fat.

The contribution of milk to dietary fat intake is decreasing as more of us turn to skimmed and semi-skimmed milk. Eggs provide a significant source of fat in many human diets. However, they are also an excellent source of high biological value protein and essential vitamins (A, D and folic acid) and minerals such as zinc and selenium.

The story on fat has one interesting twist. A number of polyunsaturated fats that occur in plants and fish oils are thought to be particularly beneficial to health. They include Docosahexaenoic Acid (DHA) and Eicosapentaenoic Acid (EPA), which are classified as omega-3 fatty acids, and Gamma Linolenic Acid (GLA), an omega-6 fatty acid. These fatty acids are required in very small quantities but both types are necessary for the structure and functions of body cells.

Oily fish such as herring, mackerel, pilchards, salmon, sardines, trout and tuna represent the principal sources of omega-3 fatty acids. Omega-3 fish oils may help to prevent heart disease by decreasing the tendency of the blood to clot and stabilizing the cell membranes of the heart. Current government recommendations suggest that the average intake of omega-3 for the general population should be doubled. This can easily be achieved by increasing consumption of oily fish to about once or twice a week. At the same time, a decrease in total fat intake and specifically saturated fats is recommended.

Linolenic (omega-6) acid is obtained in the diet mainly from seeds and polyunsaturated margarines. Commercially available supplements such as evening primrose and starflower supply appreciable amounts of GLA, while linseed oil contains both omega-3 and omega-6 and therefore makes a good supplement for those who cannot take fish oils.

Water

Water is vital. Adults can survive for many weeks without food but only a few days without water. Water comprises about two-thirds of the body's weight and is the medium in which almost all body processes take place. Water is lost from the body by evaporation in the breath, sweat and urine. Most adults need about 2 litres/3½ pints of water a day – more if heavy physical work or exercise is performed. Some water is obtained from other fluids and even from solid foods. However, both caffeine (in hot drinks such as tea and coffee) and alcohol (in wine and beer) affect the body's ability to use water, and should never be thought of as replacing pure water.

Vitamins and minerals

Vitamins and minerals are essential to health. Vitamins are only needed in minute amounts, which will be found in a balanced diet that contains a wide variety of fresh foods. Vitamins are divided into two groups: the fat-soluble vitamins A, D, E and K; and the water-soluble B-complex vitamins and vitamin C. Minerals can be sub-divided into major minerals (macrominerals) and trace elements (microminerals). Macrominerals are those present in the largest amounts in the body's tissues. They include calcium, iron, magnesium, phosphorus, sodium, potassium, chloride and zinc. Microminerals are equally important but are needed in minute quantities. They include copper, selenium, iodine, manganese, chromium and fluoride. Some minerals (calcium, phosphorus, magnesium) are important constituents of bones and teeth. Others (such as iron) are essential adjuncts to enzymes and other protein molecules, such as haemoglobin, which transports oxygen in the blood. Minerals also help to regulate body composition and fluid balance.

The only way to ensure their supply in the right amount and correct proportions is to consume a balanced, varied diet. Different foods contain a mixture of nutrients in various quantities. To prevent or manage a problem like osteoporosis ('brittle bone disease'), for example, one needs an adequate consumption of not only calcium but also of all the minerals and vitamins that help in the absorption and metabolism of calcium (magnesium, phosphorus, silica, iron, vitamin D, vitamin K).

People with poor eating habits and those who follow a restricted diet may lack certain vitamins, but severe vitamin deficiency, which causes diseases such as rickets and scurvy, is rarely found in modern societies. However, subclinical deficiency, which can only be detected via a blood test, is not uncommon and could be responsible for a number of the degenerative diseases of today. It is important to seek advice from a doctor or qualified nutritionist before taking a vitamin or mineral supplement to avoid duplication. While high intakes of the water-soluble vitamins, albeit not desirable, have little effect on the body as they are rapidly excreted in the urine, excessive intakes of the fat-soluble vitamin A can be dangerous as it accumulates in the body. Most minerals can also be toxic, or at least cause some health problems, if taken in excess. Once you start taking multi-vitamin and mineral supplements the amounts can add up. Look at your diet before turning to supplements.

The antioxidants

Research is continuing to uncover the exciting properties of certain compounds, the antioxidants. Beta-carotene (a vegetable form of vitamin A), vitamin C, vitamin E, zinc and selenium are among the many compounds in food that have antioxidant properties. Antioxidants help to counter the damaging effects of reactive oxygen molecules – called free radicals.

Free radicals are produced as part of the body's normal metabolic processes, but are generally scavenged and disposed of by the body's sophisticated defence system. If they accumulate they can cause cell damage, and damaged cells may be more prone to developing cancer. Another harmful effect of free radicals is the oxidation of LDL cholesterol, which may play a part in the formation of the 'plaque' that can build up on the walls of the blood vessels, leading to thickening and narrowing of the arteries and eventually to raised blood pressure and heart disease.

People who consume appreciable quantities of orange and yellow fruits and dark green or orange vegetables (which are rich in beta-carotene) seem to be less prone to some forms of cancer. Beta-carotene may play a role in boosting the body's natural defence mechanism against cancer by helping to destroy free-radicals and regenerating vitamin E. Vitamin C seems to work in a similar way. Alpha-tocopherol (vitamin E), the most potent of antioxidant vitamins, can help prevent the formation of free radicals and the oxidation of LDL cholesterol. Other antioxidant compounds are continually being discovered, including flavonoids such as those found in red wine, broccoli and tomatoes. Antioxidants appear to work in a very sophisticated manner with one complementing the role of another. This again illustrates the importance of a varied, balanced diet.

adopting a healthy lifestyle

Champneys addresses the whole individual: we hope that our guests will leave us feeling replenished in mind, body and soul. We also hope that they will be inspired to continue the healthy lifestyle programme we have established, taking time to exercise, relax and eat healthily.

A simple visual reminder of healthy eating guidelines is found on the Champneys plate. This illustrates what to aim for in each day's dishes, menus and meals, in terms of food groups, and shows how you can plan a balanced diet. Bearing this image in mind should help you select sensibly not only while you are a guest at Champneys, but also when you are cooking at home or eating out. Individuals differ in the amount of food they need and the foods they like, but the proportions of food from each group should remain the same (unless there is a specific health requirement).

To keep your weight steady while adjusting to a healthier way of eating, envisage the weight maintenance plate (shown right): 33% carbohydrate – complex carbohydrates (starchy foods) keep the body supplied with energy; 33% protein; 33% fruit and vegetables – high in fibre, low in fat and rich in vitamins and minerals. Current healthy eating guidelines recommend that at least five to eight servings of fruits and vegetables should be eaten each day. (They can be fresh or frozen, or even tinned fruit, as long as it is in natural juice rather than syrup.)

If you are trying to lose weight, adjust the proportions of these food groups to 25% complex carbohydrates, 25% protein and 50% fruit and vegetables. Changing the proportions in this way reduces total energy intake (calories) without affecting the nutritional value of the meal. We call this the light diet or weight management plate.

Increasing your intake of fruits, vegetables and starchy foods is the best way to reduce the fat in your

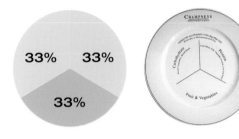

Weight maintenance plate

- Carbohydrate
  Starchy foods: bread, pasta, rice, oats and other cereals, polenta, couscous, cracked wheat, potatoes

- Protein
  Lean meat, poultry, game, fish, eggs, dairy products, lentils, beans

- Fruit and vegetables

diet. This is where Champneys coding can help. Whether you are staying at Champneys or enjoying some of the recipes in this book, all you have to do is count the hearts. To maintain a steady weight, women should keep to 12 or 13 hearts a day, men to about 16 hearts. If you want to lose weight, reduce the number of hearts slightly. Ideally most of this should be unsaturated fat (see page 16).

Champneys can give you a wonderful sense of vitality; use this book to renew that feeling of glowing health.

Dr Asma B. Omer *(BSc, SRD, MSc, PhD)*
Head of Nutrition and Dietetics Department

recipes 2

breakfasts

Make time for breakfast and wake up to a burst of energy. Fruits and cereals are not only quick and colourful, they also provide a perfect package of vitamins and carbohydrates. Add protein in the form of dairy products, eggs or fish and give your day a great new beginning.

apple, walnut, date and apricot loaf

Heat the oven to 170°C/325°F/gas 3. Line a 1 litre/1¾ pint loaf tin with greaseproof paper.

Put the sugar and eggs into a large bowl, place over a saucepan of gently simmering water and whisk until light and fluffy. Add the olive oil spread and beat in. Do not let the mixture get too hot or the eggs will scramble.

Mix the flour, salt and baking powder together, sift into the egg mixture and fold in with a metal spoon (reserve the bran residue left in the sieve). Fold in the walnuts, apricots, dates and apples and pour into the lined loaf tin. Sprinkle the bran residue over the top.

Bake for 1 hour 10 minutes. To test, insert a skewer into the centre of the loaf; if it comes out clean the loaf is cooked, otherwise return the loaf to the oven for about 5 minutes, then test again. Turn out on to a wire rack and leave to cool. When cold, slice and serve. This loaf can be made a day ahead; store in an airtight container.

Champneys rating

SERVES 12

140 g/5 oz **sugar**

2 **eggs**

90 g/3 oz **olive oil spread**

240 g/8½ oz **wholemeal flour**

pinch of **salt**

1½ teaspoons **baking powder**

100 g/3½ oz **walnuts**, chopped

70 g/2½ oz **dried apricots**, chopped

50 g/2 oz **dried dates**, chopped

225 g/8 oz **cooking apples**, peeled, cored and diced

champneys fresh yoghurt muesli

Put the oats, oatbran and wheatgerm in a large bowl, add enough milk to cover and leave to soak overnight in the refrigerator.

In the morning, add all the remaining ingredients and mix together, stirring in the delicate berry fruits last. Serve in bowls or elegant glasses and decorate with sprigs of mint.

Champneys rating

SERVES 4

2 tablespoons **rolled oats**

1 tablespoon **oatbran**

1 tablespoon **wheatgerm**

about 100 ml/3½ fl oz **skimmed milk**

2 tablespoons **chopped mixed nuts**

3 **dried apricots**, chopped

1 **red apple**, coarsely grated

1 **green apple**, coarsely grated

1 **banana**, diced

grated zest of 1 **orange**

200 ml/7 fl oz **low-fat greek yoghurt**

1 tablespoon **maple syrup**

200 g/7 oz **fresh berries**

sprigs of **mint**, to decorate

bulgar wheat, apple, pear and cinnamon muesli

Put the bulgar wheat, sugar, cinnamon, ginger, orange zest and juice and soya milk in a small saucepan. Bring to the boil and simmer until the bulgar wheat has absorbed all the milk. Leave to cool and then mix with the almonds and diced apples and pear.

Put the honey and blackcurrants in a small saucepan, boil for 2 minutes, then leave to cool.

Serve the muesli in bowls and spoon the blackcurrants on top. Add a few more almonds, sprinkle with icing sugar and decorate with sprigs of mint.

Champneys rating

SERVES 4

50 g/2 oz **bulgar wheat**

50 g/2 oz **sugar**

1 teaspoon **ground cinnamon**

½ teaspoon **ground ginger**

grated zest and juice of 1 **orange**

200 ml/7 fl oz **soya milk**

40 g/1½ oz whole **almonds**,
    plus extra to serve

1 **red apple**, diced

1 **green apple**, diced

1 ripe **pear**, diced

2 tablespoons **clear honey**

100 g/3½ oz **blackcurrants**

icing sugar and sprigs of **mint**,
    to decorate

potato and chive cakes
with poached eggs and smoked salmon

To make the potato cakes, mix the mashed potato with the flour, chives and crushed coriander seeds. Season to taste with salt and pepper and mix to form a firm dough. Roll out on a lightly floured surface to a thickness of about 5 mm/¼ inch. Using a 7 cm/2¾ inch cutter, cut out 8 cakes. Heat the oil in a non-stick frying pan and cook the potato cakes until lightly browned, about 3 minutes on each side.

Half-fill a wide, shallow pan with water, add the vinegar and bring to the boil. Reduce the heat to a gentle simmer and poach the eggs for 3 minutes or until softly poached. Lift out with a slotted spoon and drain on kitchen paper.

Serve 2 potato cakes per person, with the poached eggs on top and a twist of smoked salmon on the side. Grind black pepper and squeeze a little lemon juice over the salmon. Garnish with parsley.

Champneys rating

SERVES 4

1 tablespoon **white wine vinegar**

4 **eggs**

4 slices of **smoked salmon**
    (about 170 g/6 oz total weight)

1 **lemon**, halved

flat-leaf parsley, to garnish

potato cakes

250 g/9 oz cooked mashed **potato**

50 g/2 oz **wholemeal flour**

3 tablespoons chopped **chives**

1 teaspoon crushed **coriander seeds**

salt and freshly ground **black pepper**

1 tablespoon **groundnut**
    or **grapeseed oil**

banana, citrus and oat smoothie

Put the oats in a bowl, add the milk and leave to soak overnight in the refrigerator. Keep the fruit, yoghurt and fromage frais in the refrigerator overnight.

In the morning, chop the bananas and place in a blender with all the remaining ingredients. Blend until smooth, then pass through a fine sieve and serve in iced glasses, with more ice and straws.

Champneys rating

SERVES 4

50 g/2 oz **rolled oats**

100 ml/3½ fl oz **skimmed milk**

3 small **bananas**

finely grated zest and juice of 1 **orange**

finely grated zest and juice of 1 **lemon**

150 ml/5 fl oz **low-fat yoghurt**

150 ml/5 fl oz **low-fat fromage frais**

3 tablespoons **clear honey**

pinch of **mixed spice**

8 **ice cubes**

soups

With their glorious colours and unexpected flavours, it is no wonder that soups are perennial favourites on the Champneys menu.

roasted corn and sweet potato soup

with tortilla chips

Heat the oven to 200°C/400°F/gas 6. Brush the oil over a baking sheet, add the sweetcorn and diced potato and roast until golden brown, about 20 minutes. Remove from the oven and set aside a quarter of the sweetcorn and potato mixture for the garnish.

In a thick-bottomed saucepan, simmer the stock, milk, onions, celery, garlic, lime leaves, bay leaf and cumin until the vegetables are tender, about 20 minutes.

For the garnish, mix the lime zest with the paprika and then roll the reserved sweetcorn and potato in the paprika mixture.

Remove the bay leaf and lime leaves from the stock and vegetables. Add the sweetcorn and potato mixture (not the garnish) and liquidize until smooth. Add the juice of 1–2 limes, to taste, and season with salt and pepper. Pass through a sieve and reheat gently. Serve in warmed soup bowls, stir in the garnish and crumble the tortilla chips on top.

Champneys rating

SERVES 4

1 tablespoon **grapeseed oil**

250 g/9 oz **sweetcorn kernels**

250 g/9 oz **sweet potato**, cut into
   1 cm/½ inch dice

500 ml/16 fl oz **chicken** or
   vegetable stock

100 ml/3½ fl oz **skimmed milk**

2 **onions**, chopped

2 sticks **celery**, chopped

2 **garlic cloves**

4 **kaffir lime leaves**

1 **bay leaf**

½ teaspoon **ground cumin**

finely grated zest of 1 **lime** and juice
   of 1–2 **limes**

1 teaspoon **smoked paprika**
   (or regular paprika)

salt and freshly ground **black pepper**

10 **tortilla chips**

chilled roasted vegetable soup

with bread cannelloni

Heat the oven to 190°C/375°F/gas 5. Put the aubergine, tomatoes, courgettes, red pepper, onion, leek and garlic in a non-stick roasting tin. Liquidize the wine with the olive oil, lemon juice and sugar and then mix with the vegetables. Roast for 20–25 minutes.

When the vegetables are tender, put them into a liquidizer with the tomato juice, half the basil, parsley, Worcestershire sauce and anchovy essence and blend until smooth. Season to taste with salt and pepper and then pass through a sieve and refrigerate for at least 2 hours, or overnight.

To make the bread cannelloni, heat the oven to 190°C/375°F/gas 5. Roll the bread through a pasta machine or roll out with a rolling pin, then cut each slice in half. Mix the tomato, anchovies, olives and herbs and place a little of the mixture on each piece of bread. Roll up and pinch the ends to seal, then place on a non-stick baking sheet, brush lightly with olive oil and bake for 15 minutes. Serve the chilled soup in soup plates, sprinkled with the remaining basil and accompanied by the warm cannelloni.

Champneys rating

SERVES 4

120 g/4 oz **aubergine**, peeled, diced

300 g/11 oz **tomatoes**, cut into
    quarters, seeds removed

120 g/4 oz **courgettes**, roughly diced

1 **red pepper**, deseeded and
    roughly diced

1 large **onion**, roughly chopped

1 small **leek**, roughly chopped

2 **garlic cloves**, peeled

100 ml/3½ fl oz **dry white wine**

1 tablespoon **olive oil**

juice of ½ **lemon**

1 teaspoon **caster sugar**

400 ml/14 fl oz **tomato juice**

2 teaspoons chopped **basil**

1 teaspoon chopped **parsley**

1 dash **worcestershire sauce**

1 dash **anchovy essence**

salt and **pepper**

bread cannelloni

4 slices **white bread**, crusts removed

1 **beefsteak tomato**, skinned,
    deseeded and finely diced

4 **anchovy fillets**, finely chopped

6 **olives**, finely chopped

1 teaspoon chopped **chives**

4 **basil leaves**, chopped

2 teaspoons **olive oil** for brushing

fresh herb soup

with green and broad beans

Put the milk, bay leaves and cloves in a thick-bottomed saucepan and warm over a low heat, without boiling, for about 20 minutes.

Remove the bay leaves and cloves and add the leek, onions, potatoes, celery and garlic. Bring to simmering point, cover and simmer for 20–30 minutes until the vegetables are very soft.

Add the basil leaves and liquidize the soup, then pass through a sieve. Whisk in the fromage frais and then stir in the green beans, broad beans and herbs. Season to taste with salt and pepper. To serve, reheat gently, without boiling, and serve in soup plates.

Champneys rating

SERVES 4

750 ml/1¼ pints **semi-skimmed milk**

2 **bay leaves**

2 **cloves**

1 **leek** (white part only), sliced

2 **onions**, sliced

2 **potatoes**, peeled and chopped

2 sticks **celery**, sliced

2 **garlic cloves**

1 bunch **basil**

2 tablespoons **low-fat fromage frais**

20 **green beans**, blanched and finely sliced

60 **broad beans**, blanched and peeled

6 tablespoons very finely chopped **chives, chervil** and **parsley**

salt and **pepper**

parsnip, honey and mustard soup

Put the parsnips, onions, leek, celery, garlic, coriander seeds and bay leaves in a thick-bottomed saucepan, add the stock and boil for about 20–30 minutes until all the vegetables are tender.

Remove the bay leaves, then liquidize the soup and add the milk, mustard, honey and lemon juice. Season to taste with salt and pepper, then pass through a sieve. To serve, reheat and serve in bowls, sprinkled with the chopped parsley.

Champneys rating

SERVES 4

500 g/1 lb 2 oz **parsnips**, peeled and chopped

2 **onions**, chopped

1 **leek**, chopped

3 sticks **celery**

2 **garlic cloves**

½ teaspoon crushed **coriander seeds**

2 **bay leaves**

750 ml/1¼ pints **vegetable stock**

150 ml/5 fl oz **semi-skimmed milk**

1 teaspoon **wholegrain mustard**

1 teaspoon **honey**

juice of ½ **lemon**

salt and **pepper**

1 tablespoon chopped **parsley**, to garnish

clear chicken soup

with chicken, prawn and ginger dim sum

To make the dim sum, mix the garlic, ginger, plum sauce, soy sauce, fish sauce, chilli powder, five-spice powder, half the chopped spring onions and the ½ egg white together in a bowl. Stir in the chopped chicken and prawns. Leave to marinate in the refrigerator for 1–2 hours.

Soak the noodles or cook them according to the packet instructions. Drain on kitchen paper. To shape the dim sum, roll the chicken and prawn mixture into small, walnut-sized balls; you will need 12 in total. Lay out 6 or 7 noodles side by side and cut into 20 cm/8 inch lengths. Roll each chicken and prawn ball over the top of the noodles so that the ball is wrapped in noodles. Keep on a tray in the refrigerator until ready to use.

For the soup, put the chicken stock in a saucepan with 1 teaspoon of the soy sauce and the rice wine and bring to the boil. Heat the sesame oil in a wok or non-stick frying pan and stir-fry the vegetables, adding a splash or two of water to prevent sticking. Add to the soup and boil for 2 minutes. Taste the soup and add a little more soy sauce if you like.

To serve, steam the dim sum in a bamboo steamer over a saucepan of boiling water for 3–4 minutes. Ladle the soup and vegetables into soup bowls. Add 3 steamed dim sum to each plate, sprinkle with the remaining spring onions and serve hot.

Champneys rating

SERVES 4

750 ml/1¼ pints **chicken stock**

1–2 teaspoons **soy sauce**

1 teaspoon **rice wine**

1 teaspoon **sesame oil**

25 g/1 oz **beansprouts**

2 **pak choi**, shredded

1 **carrot**, cut into fine strips

8 fresh **shiitake mushrooms**, sliced

dim sum

1 **garlic clove**, crushed

1 teaspoon grated **fresh ginger**

1 teaspoon each of **plum sauce,**
    soy sauce and **thai fish sauce**

pinch of **chilli powder**

pinch of **five-spice powder**

1 bunch **spring onions**, chopped

½ **egg white**

200 g/7 oz **chicken breast**, skin
    removed, finely chopped

90 g/3 oz cooked **prawns**,
    finely chopped

90 g/3 oz **fine egg noodles**

lentil, lime and coriander soup
with mint and chilli yoghurt

Put the Puy lentils in a saucepan, cover with cold water and bring to the boil. Cook for 20 minutes until tender, then drain and set aside. Cook the red lentils in a separate saucepan for 15 minutes, then drain.

In a large saucepan, dry-sweat the celery, onion, carrot, red pepper and garlic over a low heat, stirring constantly for 5 minutes. Then add the stock, bay leaves, lime zest, lime pickle, tomato purée and the cooked red lentils. Bring to a simmer and cook over a low heat for 30 minutes until all the vegetables are tender. Remove the bay leaves. Add the coriander leaves and liquidize until smooth, then pass through a sieve into another pan.

Add the cooked Puy lentils and season to taste with the lime juice, salt and pepper. Mix the yoghurt with the mint and sweet chilli sauce. To serve, gently reheat the soup and serve in warmed bowls, with the mint and chilli yoghurt on top.

Champneys rating

SERVES 4

25 g/1 oz **puy lentils**

140 g/5 oz **red split lentils**

4 sticks **celery**, roughly chopped

1 large **onion**, roughly chopped

1 **carrot**, roughly chopped

1 **red pepper**, deseeded and roughly chopped

2 **garlic cloves**

500 ml/16 fl oz **vegetable stock**

3 **bay leaves**

finely grated zest and juice of 1 **lime**

½ teaspoon **lime pickle** (just the liquid)

2 tablespoons **tomato purée**

1 small bunch **coriander**

salt and **pepper**

2 tablespoons **low-fat greek yoghurt**

1 teaspoon chopped **mint** or

¼ teaspoon **mint sauce concentrate** or

1 teaspoon **mint jelly**

½ teaspoon **sweet chilli sauce**

carrot, peanut, orange and sesame soup

Heat the oven to 200°C/400°F/gas 6. Roast the carrots, onions, leek, celery and garlic in a non-stick roasting tin for 20 minutes until golden brown.

Transfer the roasted vegetables to a saucepan and add the stock, orange juice, butter beans, milk, bay leaf and tarragon. Bring to the boil and simmer for 10–15 minutes. Add the orange zest, peanut butter and tahini.

Liquidize until smooth and then pass through a sieve. Serve in bowls, sprinkled with the sesame seeds.

Champneys rating

SERVES 4

500 g/1 lb 2 oz **carrots**, roughly chopped

2 small **onions**, roughly chopped

1 **leek**, roughly chopped

4 sticks **celery**, roughly chopped

2 **garlic cloves**

750 ml/1¼ pints **chicken** or **vegetable stock**

finely grated zest and juice of 1 **orange**

100 g/3½ oz cooked **butter beans**

100 ml/3½ fl oz **semi-skimmed milk**

1 **bay leaf**

1 teaspoon chopped **tarragon**

2 tablespoons **peanut butter**

1 teaspoon **tahini**

½ teaspoon **sesame seeds**, toasted

smoked haddock, scallop and leek chowder

Cook 200 g/7 oz of the potato in boiling salted water until just overcooked, then liquidize with the scallop corals. Cut the scallops into slices and set aside.

Heat a non-stick frying pan over low heat, add the olive oil, onion, leeks and remaining potato and cook until soft but not browned. Add the smoked haddock and cook for 2 minutes, then add the vermouth and simmer to reduce by two-thirds. Add the saffron, milk and fish stock and stir in the potato purée. Bring to a simmer and cook for 15 minutes on a low heat.

To serve, stir in the crème fraîche and lemon juice, then season to taste with salt and pepper and serve in warmed soup plates. Heat a non-stick frying pan over a high heat; when it is very hot, sear the scallops for 10 seconds on each side, then add to the soup and serve at once, sprinkled with chives.

Champneys rating

SERVES 4

300 g/11 oz **potatoes**, peeled and diced

4 **king scallops**, corals removed and reserved

1 tablespoon **olive oil**

1 **onion**, finely diced

2 **leeks**, finely diced

300 g/11 oz **undyed smoked haddock**

50 ml/2 fl oz **dry vermouth**

pinch of **saffron strands**

500 ml/16 fl oz **semi-skimmed milk**

500 ml/16 fl oz **fish stock**

3 tablespoons **low-fat crème fraîche**

1 **lemon**

salt and **pepper**

1 tablespoon snipped **chives**, to garnish

roasted pumpkin soup

with pumpkin seed pesto

Heat the oven to 200°C/400°F/gas 6. Peel, deseed and roughly cube the pumpkin or squash, reserving the seeds. Spread the pumpkin and seeds on separate non-stick baking sheets and roast in the hot oven; turn the seeds after 5 minutes and continue roasting until golden brown. Leave to cool. (Alternatively you could use 2–3 tablespoons bought roasted pumpkin seeds.) Roast the pumpkin for 20 minutes or until tender.

Put the milk and vegetable stock in a thick-bottomed saucepan. Add the onions, celery, carrots, bay leaves and 2 garlic cloves and bring to the boil. Simmer for 15–20 minutes until the vegetables are soft and pulpy.

Reserving a few for garnish, grind the roasted seeds in a spice grinder or mortar and pestle together with the ginger and remaining garlic. Add the basil and Parmesan and blend until it forms a smooth paste. Season to taste with salt and pepper and keep in a warm place.

Remove the bay leaves from the stock and add three-quarters of the roasted pumpkin. Liquidize until smooth, then pass through a sieve into a clean saucepan. Reheat and season to taste with lime juice, salt and pepper. Serve in soup plates, with the remaining roasted pumpkin, a little pumpkin seed pesto and a few roasted pumpkin seeds on top.

Champneys rating

SERVES 4

1 kg/2¼ lb **pumpkin** or
    butternut squash

250 ml/8 fl oz **semi-skimmed milk**

250 ml/8 fl oz **vegetable stock**

2 **onions**, 2 sticks **celery** and
    2 **carrots**, roughly chopped

2 **bay leaves**

3 **garlic cloves**

½ teaspoon grated **fresh ginger**

½ bunch **basil**, leaves only

1 teaspoon freshly grated **parmesan**
    cheese

salt and **pepper**

juice of 1–2 **limes**

mushroom, butter bean and tarragon soup

In a thick-bottomed non-stick saucepan, dry-sweat the onions and garlic until golden brown. Add the dried and fresh mushrooms, the milk, bay leaf and butter beans and simmer for 20 minutes.

Add three-quarters of the tarragon, then liquidize the soup until smooth and pass through a sieve. Whisk in half the fromage frais, season to taste with salt and pepper and reheat gently.

Chop the remaining tarragon very finely, then mix with the remaining fromage frais. Pour the hot soup into warmed bowls and swirl in the tarragon fromage frais.

Champneys rating

SERVES 4

2 large **onions**, sliced

2 **garlic cloves**, crushed

25 g/1 oz **dried ceps**
  (porcini mushrooms)

120 g/4 oz **flat field mushrooms**

500 ml/16 fl oz **semi-skimmed milk**

1 **bay leaf**

400 g/14 oz cooked **butter beans**

1 small bunch **tarragon**, leaves only

2 tablespoons **fromage frais**

salt and **pepper**

tomato consommé
with grilled goats' cheese
and smoked salmon

Heat the oven to 200°C/400°F/gas 6. Roast the tomato quarters on a baking sheet for 15 minutes, then liquidize with the vegetable stock and star anise. Leave to cool.

Mix the finely diced vegetables with the bay leaves, egg whites, minced smoked salmon, fish sauce and basil. Stir in the cooled tomato mixture and put into a saucepan over a low heat. Gently warm; do not boil. The egg white mixture will rise to form a 'crust'. When the soup has reached a very gentle simmer, remove from the heat and leave to stand for 15 minutes. Very carefully break the crust and ladle out the soup. Put the soup, a ladleful at a time, through a sieve lined with a coffee filter into a clean saucepan. Do not put the egg white clarification through the sieve.

To serve, heat the grill to very hot. Grill the goats' cheese until it is golden brown. Meanwhile, gently reheat the soup, check the seasoning, then pour into soup plates. Drop in the smoked salmon diamonds, diced tomatoes and chives, then carefully add a slice of grilled goats' cheese to each bowl.

Champneys rating

SERVES 4

2 kg/4½ lb over-ripe **tomatoes**, cut into
   quarters, seeds removed

1 litre/1¾ pints **vegetable stock**

2 **star anise**

1 **carrot**, 1 **onion**, 2 sticks **celery**,
   1 **leek**, 1 **garlic clove**, all finely diced

2 **bay leaves**

3 **egg whites**

50 g/2 oz **smoked salmon**, minced

1 tablespoon **thai fish sauce**

1 bunch **sweet basil**, finely chopped

salt and **pepper**

to serve

50 g/2 oz firm **goats' cheese**, cut into
   1 cm/½ inch slices

25 g/1 oz **smoked salmon**, cut into
   diamond shapes

2 **tomatoes**, skinned, deseeded
   and diced

1 tablespoon snipped **chives**

chickpea, tomato and noodle soup

In a large, thick-bottomed, non-stick saucepan, dry-sweat the onions and garlic until golden brown. Add half the chickpeas, half the tomatoes, 1 red pepper, the tomato purée, cumin, coriander seeds, turmeric, paprika and cinnamon. Add the stock and bring to the boil. Simmer for 20 minutes.

Mix the remaining chickpeas, tomatoes and red pepper together in a saucepan and gently warm over a low heat with the balsamic vinegar and sugar.

Add half the basil to the soup and liquidize until smooth, then pass through a sieve and reheat gently.

Cut the noodles into 5 cm/2 inch pieces and cook in boiling water until tender, then strain. Mix the noodles with the chickpea and balsamic vinegar mixture and ladle into soup bowls. Season the soup with lemon juice, salt and pepper to taste and pour over the noodles and chickpeas. Sprinkle with the remaining basil and serve with lemon wedges.

Champneys rating

SERVES 4

2 **onions**, sliced

3 **garlic cloves**, crushed

400 g/14 oz cooked **chickpeas**

400 g/14 oz ripe **tomatoes**, skinned, deseeded and diced

2 large **red peppers**, roasted, deseeded, skinned and diced

1 tablespoon **tomato purée**

1 teaspoon **ground cumin**

1 teaspoon crushed **coriander seeds**

1 teaspoon **turmeric**

1 teaspoon **sweet paprika**

½ teaspoon **ground cinnamon**

500 ml/16 fl oz **vegetable stock**

1 tablespoon **balsamic vinegar**

1 teaspoon **soft brown sugar**

1 small bunch **basil**, leaves only, chopped

100 g/3½ oz **egg noodles**

juice of 1 **lemon**

1 **lemon**, cut into wedges, to serve

jerusalem artichoke, garlic and lemon soup

Heat the oven to 190°C/375°F/gas 5. Put the garlic cloves in a small roasting tin and roast for 20 minutes. Pop the cloves out of their skins.

In a large saucepan, boil the artichokes with the potatoes, onions, celery, roasted garlic, lemon thyme, 1 teaspoon sugar and the stock until the artichokes are tender, about 20–25 minutes.

Remove the pan from the heat and add the lemon juice and fromage frais, and season to taste with a little salt and pepper. Liquidize until smooth, then pass through a sieve. Mix the lemon zest and yoghurt together with the remaining sugar. Reheat the soup and serve with the lemon yoghurt and garlic chives on top.

Champneys rating

SERVES 4

8 **garlic cloves**, in their skins

400 g/14 oz **jerusalem artichokes**, peeled and chopped

140 g/5 oz **potatoes**, peeled and diced

2 small **onions**, roughly chopped

3 sticks **celery**, roughly chopped

pinch of **lemon thyme**

2 teaspoons **caster sugar**

500 ml/16 fl oz **vegetable stock**

grated zest of 2 **lemons**, juice of 1 **lemon**

2 tablespoons **low-fat fromage frais**

salt and **pepper**

1 tablespoon **low-fat yoghurt**

8 **garlic chives**

right: Red onion soup with parmesan choux

red onion soup
with parmesan choux

Heat the oven to 200°C/400°F/gas 6. For the vegetable stock, put the celery, fennel, carrots, onions, tomatoes and garlic cloves into a roasting tin and roast for 20 minutes. Transfer the roasted vegetables to a large saucepan and add the remaining stock ingredients and 2 litres/3½ pints water. Simmer, uncovered, for 1¼ hours. Strain the liquid into a measuring jug; you should end up with about 750 ml/1¼ pints stock.

In a large, thick-bottomed saucepan, dry-sweat the onions over a very low heat. You do not need to add any oil, but you must stir continuously for the first 5–10 minutes. Continue cooking for a further 20 minutes, stirring occasionally, so that they caramelize.

Meanwhile, make the Parmesan choux. Heat the oven to 200°C/400°F/gas 6. Put the olive oil spread and 125 ml/4 fl oz water in a saucepan over medium heat. When the spread melts, add the flour and whisk over the heat for 2 minutes. Gradually beat in the eggs, a little at a time, beat in the salt, then pipe into four oiled 6 cm/2¼ inch cutters on a baking sheet and bake for 20 minutes until the choux are risen and golden brown. Sprinkle the Parmesan and chives over the hot choux.

When the onions are cooked and golden brown, but not burnt, add the red wine and balsamic vinegar, turn up the heat and allow the liquid to evaporate completely. Add the vegetable stock, simmer for 5 minutes, then stir in the mustard and season to taste with salt and pepper. Serve in bowls, with a Parmesan choux on top.

Champneys rating

SERVES 4

10 **red onions**, finely sliced

100 ml/3½ fl oz **red wine**

2 tablespoons **balsamic vinegar**

1 tablespoon **dijon mustard**

salt and **pepper**

vegetable stock

1 head of **celery**, 1 **fennel bulb**,
    5 **carrots**, 4 **onions**, diced

4 **tomatoes**, cut in half,
    seeds removed

4 **garlic cloves**

10 **parsley stalks**

10 **dried ceps** (porcini mushrooms)

2 **star anise**

4 **bay leaves**

1 tablespoon **coriander seeds**

1 tablespoon **fennel seeds**

parmesan choux

40 g/1½ oz **olive oil spread**

70 g/2½ oz **flour**, sifted on to a piece
    of greaseproof paper

2 **eggs**, beaten

pinch of **salt**

25 g/1 oz **parmesan** cheese,
    finely grated

1 tablespoon chopped **chives**

starters

A first course should appeal to the eye and excite the palate in anticipation of the meal to follow. Many of the starters in this chapter would also make fabulous lunch or supper dishes.

onion bhaji
with spinach, curd cheese and mango

First make the fruit raita, peel and dice all of the fruit, then mix with the yoghurt, chilli, saffron, sugar and onion. Keep in the refrigerator. If the raita becomes too thin, place a piece of muslin or a clean tea towel in a sieve, put the mixture in the sieve and leave to strain in the refrigerator.

Heat the oven to 180°C/350°F/gas 4. To make the bhaji, mix the spices with the flour. Stir the curry paste with the oil, onions and garlic and then stir in the flour mixture and the fresh coriander. Divide the mixture into 12 pieces, place on a non-stick baking sheet and then flatten with a palette knife so that each piece is about 5 cm/2 inches across. Bake for 20 minutes; keep warm.

In a large saucepan with a tight-fitting lid, bring 3 tablespoons water to the boil. Add a little salt, then add the spinach, replace the lid and cook over high heat for 4 minutes, stirring occasionally. When cooked, strain and squeeze out in a clean tea towel to remove all the excess water. Add the cheese and mango chutney and season to taste with salt and pepper.

To serve, layer the spinach mixture between the onion bhaji, allowing 3 bhaji per person. Spoon a little fruit raita on to each plate and serve with freshly grilled popadoms.

Champneys rating

SERVES 4

pinch of **celery salt**

pinch of **ground coriander**

pinch of **chilli powder**

50 g/2 oz **wholemeal flour**

1 teaspoon **mild curry paste**

1 teaspoon **grapeseed oil**

300 g/11 oz **onions**, sliced

2 **garlic cloves**, crushed

3 tablespoons chopped fresh **coriander**

salt and **pepper**

1 kg/2¼ lb **young spinach**, washed

100 g/3½ oz **cottage** or **curd cheese**

1 tablespoon **mango chutney**

4 **spicy popadoms**, to serve

fruit raita

1 small **pear**, 1 small **apple**, 1 small **mango**, 1 small **banana**

100 ml/3½ fl oz **thick low-fat yoghurt**

1 small **chilli**, deseeded and diced

pinch of **saffron strands**

1 teaspoon **caster sugar**

1 small **onion**, finely chopped

stir-fried squid
with black beans, ginger and chilli

Cut the squid lengthways down one side of the body so that you can open it out flat. Using a sharp knife, lightly score in a criss-cross pattern, being careful not to cut through the skin. Trim the tentacles, discarding any hard parts. Blanch the squid and tentacles in boiling water for 1 minute; this will partly cook the squid and make it curl into tubes. Refresh in ice-cold water, then drain.

To make the marinade, mix the ginger and garlic with the black bean sauce and soaked beans (it is important that the black beans have had all the salt removed, so taste before adding them). Add the sesame oil, vinegar, lime juice, crushed coriander seeds and chilli sauce and mix thoroughly. Add the squid and marinate for at least 4 hours.

Heat a wok or large non-stick frying pan. Using a slotted spoon, lift the squid out of the marinade and stir-fry in the hot dry wok until golden brown, about 2 minutes. Add the carrots, baby corn, spring onions, curly endive and the marinade, and stir-fry for another 2 minutes.

Serve the squid on top of the vegetables, squeeze over a little lime juice and pour the cooked marinade around the outside. Scatter with sprigs of fresh coriander and serve at once.

Champneys rating

SERVES 4

12 **baby squid**, cleaned

2 **carrots**, cut into thin strips

6 **baby sweetcorn**, cut in half
   lengthways

1 bunch **spring onions**, cut diagonally
   into 3 cm/1 inch pieces

heart of a **curly endive** (frisée)

juice of ½ **lime**

1 bunch **coriander**

marinade

3 cm/1 inch piece of **fresh ginger**,
   grated

1 **garlic clove**, crushed

2 tablespoons **black bean sauce**

1 tablespoon **salted black beans**,
   rinsed and soaked in cold water for
   30 minutes

2 tablespoons **sesame oil**

3 tablespoons **rice wine vinegar**

juice of 1 **lime**

1 teaspoon **coriander seeds**,
   roasted and crushed

2 tablespoons **sweet chilli sauce**

aubergine cannelloni
with courgette and smoked salmon
and provençal sauce

Heat the oven to 190°C/375°F/gas 5. Cut the aubergines lengthways into very thin slices (about 1 mm thick), discarding the outer pieces (you should have 12 slices). Lay the slices on a baking sheet lined with baking parchment. Do the same with the courgettes. Mix the garlic with the juice of 1 lemon, the wine, 2 tablespoons olive oil, 3 teaspoons sugar, salt and pepper, blend with a hand-held blender and then brush on to the aubergine and courgette slices. Bake for 10–15 minutes until tender. While still warm lay 3 leaves of basil on each slice of aubergine and then lay a slice of courgette on top and leave to cool slightly. This will release the oils from the basil into the aubergine.

Cut the smoked salmon into strips of a similar size to the courgette slices and lay a piece of salmon on top of each. Mix the chives with the cottage cheese, fromage frais and pine nuts and season to taste with a small amount of salt and lots of black pepper. Spread on to the smoked salmon and then roll up into 12 rolls.

To make the sauce, soften the onion and garlic in the olive oil over a low heat. Add the balsamic vinegar and sugar and simmer until reduced by half. Add the passata, peppers and tomatoes and cook for 2 minutes. Season to taste with salt, pepper and a dash of sweet chilli sauce.

Whisk the remaining lemon juice with the zest, the remaining 1 tablespoon olive oil and 1 teaspoon sugar, salt and pepper to taste. Toss the spinach in the lemon vinaigrette and then sauté for 30 seconds until just beginning to wilt. Serve the aubergine cannelloni with the warm spinach and Provençal sauce. This could also be served cold.

Champneys rating

SERVES 4

2 large **aubergines**

2 **courgettes**

1 **garlic clove**, finely chopped

grated zest of ¼ **lemon**
     and juice of 1½ **lemons**

3 tablespoons **dry white wine**

3 tablespoons **olive oil**

4 teaspoons **caster sugar**

salt and freshly ground **black pepper**

36 **basil leaves**

140 g/5 oz sliced **smoked salmon**

15 g/½ oz **chives**, chopped

140 g/5 oz **cottage cheese**

3 tablespoons **fromage frais**

1 tablespoon **pine nuts**, toasted

100 g/3½ oz baby **spinach**

provençal sauce

1 **red onion**, finely chopped

½ **garlic clove**, finely chopped

1 tablespoon **olive oil**

3 tablespoons **balsamic vinegar**

1 teaspoon **caster sugar**

6 tablespoons **tomato passata**

1 **red**, 1 **green** and 1 **yellow pepper**,
     roasted, skinned, deseeded, diced

4 **tomatoes**, skinned, deseeded
     and diced

dash of **sweet chilli sauce**

stuffed cabbage leaves

with rice, sweetcorn and smoked haddock,
with curried pineapple dressing

Separate the cabbage leaves so that you have 8 similar-sized leaves. Blanch them in salted boiling water for 2 minutes, then drain and refresh under cold running water and pat dry on kitchen paper.

In a small saucepan, warm the milk with the cloves, bay leaf and onion. When warm, add the smoked haddock and simmer for 3 minutes. Using a slotted spoon, remove the haddock and flake it into the rice. Remove the bay leaves and cloves from the milk and whisk in the dissolved cornflour. Bring to the boil and cook, whisking frequently, for 1 minute. Add to the rice, together with the parsley and dill. Season to taste with cayenne and black pepper. Leave to cool.

When the mixture is cool, add the spring onions, sweetcorn, fromage frais and egg. Divide the mixture into 8 and place on the 8 cabbage leaves. Using a clean tea towel, roll the cabbage leaves around the haddock mixture to form tight balls. Trim any excess cabbage from the base, then place in a bamboo steamer ready to reheat.

To make the dressing, mix the mayonnaise and fromage frais together. Add the curry paste, chives and pineapple and mix thoroughly. Steam the cabbage balls for 5 minutes, then drain on kitchen paper. Serve with the pineapple dressing, cutting one of the cabbage balls in half on each plate.

Champneys rating

SERVES 4

1 **savoy cabbage**

150 ml/5 fl oz **skimmed milk**

4 **cloves**

1 **bay leaf**

1 small **onion**, finely chopped

100 g/3½ oz **undyed smoked haddock**

50 g/2 oz cooked **brown rice**

1 teaspoon **cornflour**, dissolved in a little water

1 teaspoon chopped **flat-leaf parsley**

1 teaspoon chopped **dill**

pinch of **cayenne pepper**

freshly ground **black pepper**

4 **spring onions**, thinly sliced

50 g/2 oz frozen **sweetcorn kernels**, thawed

1 tablespoon **fromage frais**

1 **hard-boiled egg**, chopped

curried pineapple dressing

1 tablespoon **low-fat mayonnaise**

1 tablespoon **fromage frais**

1 teaspoon **mild curry paste**

50 g/2 oz **fresh pineapple**, finely diced

10 **chives**, chopped

clams with beetroot noodles,

balsamic vinegar, broad beans and fresh herbs

Wash the clams thoroughly, discarding any with broken shells and any open clams that do not close when tapped.

Cook the beetroot in a large saucepan of salted boiling water for 30 minutes to make a strong beetroot stock. Strain into a clean saucepan and cook the noodles in the beetroot stock for 8 minutes. Refresh under cold running water and discard the stock.

Heat a thick-bottomed saucepan, add the olive oil and sweat the sliced onions over a low heat until caramelized, stirring regularly so that they do not burn.

Put the chopped onion into a large saucepan, add the balsamic vinegar and red wine and boil until reduced by half. Add the clams, cover with a tight-fitting lid and steam for 2 minutes. Remove the clams with a slotted spoon and boil the cooking liquid until caramelized. Add the caramelized sliced onions, the broad beans, fresh herbs, noodles and clams. Stir and reheat gently. Season with black pepper and serve in deep bowls.

SERVES 4

1 kg/2¼ lb **fresh clams** in shells

300 g/11 oz **raw beetroot**, peeled and chopped into 3 cm/1 inch pieces

200 g/7 oz **dried rice noodles**

1 tablespoon **olive oil**

2 **onions**, sliced

1 **onion**, finely chopped

2 tablespoons **balsamic vinegar**

4 tablespoons **red wine**

1.5 kg/3 lb **broad beans** in their pods, podded, blanched and peeled

2 tablespoons chopped **chives**

1 tablespoon chopped **chervil**

1 tablespoon chopped **basil**

freshly ground **black pepper**

Champneys rating

spicy pork spring rolls
with grilled sweetcorn

Heat the oven to 190°C/375°F/gas 5. Put the pork in a small casserole. Mix all the ingredients for the spice mixture and spread over the pork, then cover and cook for 1 hour.

Meanwhile, blanch the sweetcorn for 10 minutes in salted boiling water, then refresh in cold water. Cut the sweetcorn in half and then in half lengthways.

When the pork is cooked, remove from the spice mixture and leave to cool slightly, reserving the spice mixture. Shred the pork with a fork and season lightly with salt. Take 1 tablespoon of the spice mixture and mix with the crème fraîche and red pepper. Liquidize until smooth, then pass through a fine sieve.

Heat a wok or a deep non-stick pan. Add the vegetable oil, then stir-fry the beansprouts, carrot, red and green pepper, mangetout and spring onions for 1 minute. Drain on kitchen paper. Mix the vegetables with the shredded pork, the chickpeas and a little of the reserved spice mixture. Season to taste with salt.

Lay the spring roll pastry on a work surface, cut each sheet in half and divide the mixture between the 8 pieces of pastry. Roll up the spring rolls, tucking the ends in so that the mixture does not fall out. Place in a bamboo steamer and steam for 5 minutes.

Meanwhile, heat a griddle pan over high heat, rub the sweetcorn with a little oil, sea salt and black pepper and griddle until browned. Serve the sweetcorn with the spring rolls and a little red pepper sauce.

Champneys rating

SERVES 4

140 g/5 oz **pork fillet**, all fat and
   sinew removed

2 **sweetcorn cobs**

sea salt and freshly ground
   black pepper

2 tablespoons **low-fat crème
   fraîche**

1 **red pepper**, roasted, skinned
   deseeded and chopped

½ teaspoon **vegetable oil**

25 g/1 oz **beansprouts**

1 small **carrot**, cut into fine strips

½ **red** and ½ **green pepper**, cut into
   fine strips

10 **mangetout**, cut into fine strips

2 **spring onions**, cut into fine strips

50 g/2 oz cooked **chickpeas**

4 x 20 cm/8 inch square sheets
   spring roll pastry

spice mixture

1 teaspoon each of **ground cumin,
   ground ginger, dried oregano**

½ teaspoon each of **ground cloves,
   chilli powder, ground coriander**

2 tablespoons **tomato purée**

1 tablespoon **olive oil**

4 **garlic cloves**, crushed

grated zest and juice of 2 **limes**

crab cakes
with fruit and ginger chutney

First make the chutney; put the sherry vinegar, lime zest, orange zest and juice, shallots, sugar, ginger, garlic, chilli and spices in a stainless steel saucepan and boil until reduced to a thick syrup. Remove from the heat and stir in the diced fruits. Leave to cool.

Heat the oven to 220°C/425°F/gas 7. Bake the potato in the oven in its skin, then scoop out and mash the flesh. Reduce the oven temperature to 200°C/400°F/gas 6. When the mashed potato is cool, mix with the crab meat and diced chilli. In a separate bowl, mix the spring onions, wasabi, egg white and soy sauce. Add the crab mixture and mix thoroughly. Roll the mixture into a long sausage shape, divide into 12 pieces, then roll into individual cakes.

Mix the sesame seeds with the couscous and then roll the crab cakes in the couscous to coat them lightly. Reshape and place on a baking sheet lined with greaseproof paper. Bake for 12 minutes, turning after 6 minutes.

Stir the chopped coriander into the fruit chutney and spoon on to 4 serving plates. Lightly dress the curly endive with sesame oil and lime juice and serve with 3 warm crab cakes per person.

Champneys rating

SERVES 4

1 **potato** (about 120 g/4 oz)

140 g/5 oz **white crab meat**

1 small **green chilli**, finely diced

6 **spring onions**, diced

½ teaspoon **wasabi paste**

1 **egg white**

1 teaspoon **light soy sauce**

1 teaspoon **sesame seeds**

50 g/2 oz **couscous**

50 g/2 oz heart of **curly endive** (frisée)

1 teaspoon **dark sesame oil**

juice of 1 **lime**

fruit and ginger chutney

1 teaspoon **sherry vinegar**

grated zest of 1 **lime**

grated zest and juice of 1 **orange**

2 **shallots**, chopped

1 tablespoon **soft brown sugar**

2 teaspoons grated **fresh ginger**

1 **garlic clove**, crushed

pinch each of **chilli powder, ground cumin** and **five-spice powder**

small pinch of **ground cloves**

1 **plum**, ½ small **mango** and ½ small **apple**, cut into 5 mm/¼ inch dice

1 tablespoon chopped **fresh coriander**

carpaccio of tuna

with ginger and sesame salad

To prepare the tuna, place each steak between two pieces of lightly oiled cling film and beat gently with a rolling pin until it is 2 mm/ ⅛ inch thick – be very careful and keep turning the tuna so that you finish with a neat round shape without holes. Leave in the cling film and keep in the refrigerator until ready to serve.

Make the dressing in advance as it will improve in flavour. Whisk together the sugar, ginger, chilli and sesame oil, then stir in the toasted sesame seeds and a little sea salt.

To serve, peel one side of the cling film off the tuna and lay face down on a cold serving plate, then carefully remove the other piece of cling film. (If you like you can trim the tuna to a perfect circle using a small plate as a guide.) Squeeze the lime juice over the tuna. Dress the salad leaves and sprouts with a little of the dressing and pile in the centre of the tuna. Sprinkle the remaining dressing over the tuna.

Champneys rating

SERVES 4

4 x 70 g/2½ oz perfectly fresh **yellowfin tuna steaks**, each 2 cm/¾ inch thick

1 teaspoon **groundnut oil** for brushing cling film

½ teaspoon **caster sugar**

½ teaspoon very finely chopped **fresh ginger**

½ teaspoon very finely chopped **red** or **green chilli**

1 teaspoon **sesame oil**

1 teaspoon **sesame seeds**, toasted

sea salt

1 **lime**, halved

100 g/3½ oz mixed **curly endive** (frisée) and **sprouting beans** and **lentils** (alfalfa, mung beans, chickpeas)

smoked salmon and avocado cakes
with mustard fromage frais

Heat the oven to 190°C/375°F/gas 5. Scoop out the flesh of the potatoes and pass through a sieve into a bowl. Add the capers and parsley and then the smoked salmon, avocado and lemon juice. Season to taste with black pepper and a little salt and then mix in the beaten egg. Form into 8 balls and flatten into patty shapes with a palette knife.

Mix the chopped walnuts with the breadcrumbs and place in a shallow dish. Using a hand-held blender, whisk the walnut oil with the milk and the egg white until emulsified. Coat the cakes lightly and evenly in a little wholemeal flour, then turn them in the milk mixture and finally coat with the breadcrumbs. Place on a non-stick baking sheet and bake for 15–20 minutes until golden brown, turning after 7 minutes.

Mix the fromage frais with the lemon zest and mustard and season to taste with a little salt and pepper. Serve the hot salmon cakes with sprigs of parsley and lemon quarters. Spoon a little of the fromage frais on top.

Champneys rating

SERVES 4

400 g/14 oz **potatoes**, baked in the oven in their skins

1 teaspoon **capers**, rinsed under cold water, chopped

2 teaspoons chopped **flat-leaf parsley**, plus 4 sprigs for garnish

140 g/5 oz **smoked salmon**, chopped

1 **avocado**, diced

finely grated zest of ¼ **lemon** and juice of ½ **lemon**

sea salt and freshly ground **black pepper**

1 small **egg**, beaten

3 **walnuts**, finely chopped in a food processor

6 tablespoons **wholemeal breadcrumbs**

1½ tablespoons **walnut oil**

3 tablespoons **skimmed milk**

1 **egg white**

2 tablespoons **wholemeal flour**

3 tablespoons **fromage frais**

¼ teaspoon **wholegrain mustard**

1 **lemon**, cut into quarters for garnish

baked mushrooms
with broccoli and apricot pesto

Heat the oven to 200°C/400°F/gas 6. Place the chillies on a non-stick baking sheet and roast for 7–8 minutes; this will intensify the flavour and remove most of the heat from the chillies.

Peel the mushrooms; cut off and discard the stalks. Slice each mushroom very thinly horizontally to make 3 or 4 circular slices from each mushroom.

To make the pesto; using a sharp knife, shave the flowering tops of the broccoli, being careful not to take too much of the stalk. (You will end up with around 120 g/4 oz of broccoli tops.) Heat a small saucepan and add the garlic and broccoli tops. Cook for 30 seconds, then deglaze with the dry sherry. Remove from the heat and add the Parmesan, fromage frais and a good grinding of black pepper. Add the apricots and blend with a hand-held blender until smooth.

Reduce the oven temperature to 190°C/375°F/gas 5. Re-form the mushrooms by layering the slices with a little of the pesto, reserving some of the pesto to serve. If you like, use a large pastry cutter to trim the mushrooms to a uniform size. Place on a non-stick roasting tin and bake for 20 minutes.

Blend a quarter of the roasted chillies with the orange juice, walnut oil, tarragon mustard and fromage frais. Pass through a fine sieve. Dice the remaining chillies and mix with the diced tomatoes, corn salad and herbs.

Serve the mushrooms hot or cold. Arrange the salad in the centre of 4 plates and dress with a little of the chilli dressing. Place the mushrooms on the salad and top with a little pesto.

Champneys rating

SERVES 4

8 **fresh red chillies**, deseeded and cut into 2 cm/¾ inch pieces

4 large **flat mushrooms**

juice of ½ **orange**

2 tablespoons **walnut oil**

½ teaspoon **tarragon mustard**

1 tablespoon **fromage frais**

2 **tomatoes**, skinned, deseeded and diced

50 g/2 oz **corn salad**

15 g/½ oz mixed **fresh herbs** (chervil, coriander, flat-leaf parsley)

broccoli and apricot pesto

500 g/1 lb 2 oz **broccoli**

1 **garlic clove**, crushed

2 tablespoons **dry sherry**

2 tablespoons grated **parmesan** cheese

1 tablespoon **fromage frais**

freshly ground **black pepper**

6 **dried apricots**, chopped

smoked mackerel noodle cakes

with beetroot-asparagus salsa

First make the salsa. Chop the asparagus into 5 cm/2 inch pieces, discarding the tough stalk ends. In a non-stick saucepan, heat the olive oil and gently cook the asparagus and beetroot together. Add the sherry vinegar and cook for 1½ minutes. Remove from the heat and add the shallots, sugar, chilli powder and orange and lemon zest and juice. Finally, stir in the parsley. When the salsa is cold, season to taste with a little salt.

Heat the oven to 180°C/350°F/gas 4. Flake the smoked mackerel into a large bowl. Chop the noodles and add to the bowl, together with the lemon zest, spring onions and half the ginger and mix thoroughly. Stir in the flour and season to taste with salt and pepper. Mix the egg with about ½ tablespoon of the yoghurt and stir into the mixture. Divide the mixture into 8 balls – if the mixture is sticky, use a little more flour to coat the cakes. Press each one into a 7 cm/2¾ inch gateau ring or plain pastry cutter on a baking sheet lined with baking parchment. Spray lightly with oil and bake for 10–15 minutes until browned.

Mix the remaining yoghurt with the lemon juice and the remaining ginger and season to taste with salt and pepper.

Serve 2 noodle cakes per person on warmed plates with ½ lemon, the salsa and a little of the ginger yoghurt.

Champneys rating

SERVES 4

140 g/5 oz **smoked mackerel** fillets, skinned

120 g/4 oz **fresh egg noodles**, cooked, refreshed in cold water

grated zest and juice of 1 **lemon**

2 bunches **spring onions**, finely chopped

3 cm/1 inch piece of **fresh ginger**, grated

2 tablespoons **wholemeal flour**

salt and **pepper**

1 **egg**, lightly beaten

4 tablespoons **strained low-fat yoghurt**

cooking oil in a spray can

2 **lemons**, halved, to serve

beetroot-asparagus salsa

6 **asparagus** spears

1 tablespoon **olive oil**

50 g/2 oz **cooked beetroot**, diced

1 tablespoon **sherry vinegar**

4 **shallots**, chopped

1 tablespoon **soft brown sugar**

pinch of **chilli powder**

grated zest and juice of ½ **orange**

grated zest and juice of ½ **lemon**

1 small bunch **flat-leaf parsley**, finely chopped

potato, lamb and parma ham terrine

with fig and redcurrant compote

Heat the oven to 200°C/400°F/gas 6. Bake the potatoes in their skins until well cooked. Put the garlic in a small non-stick roasting tin and roast for 15 minutes or until golden brown.

Cut the lamb into fine strips. Heat a non-stick frying pan and when it is hot, add the lamb and seal on all sides. Line a 1 litre/1¾ pint terrine tin with the ham, leaving enough overhanging the sides to cover the top of the terrine.

It is important that you make the terrine while the potatoes are still warm; scoop out the flesh of the potatoes and layer into the terrine with the lamb and the roasted garlic. Push each layer down firmly with a fish slice so that the mixture is tightly compressed. When the mixture has filled the terrine, fold over the overhanging ham and place heavy weights on top to compress the terrine as it sets. Leave in the refrigerator for at least 2 hours, or overnight.

To make the fig and redcurrant compote, boil the figs in a little water until soft. Drain, reserving the water, pat dry and chop. Soften the shallots in a non-stick pan, adding some of the fig water to keep them moist. Then add the honey and balsamic vinegar and boil to reduce, stirring occasionally until the mixture is almost dry. Stir in the figs, redcurrants, mustard and rosemary.

To serve, turn out the terrine and wrap in cling film, then cut into 10 thick slices. Heat a non-stick frying pan over high heat and add the olive oil. Season the sliced terrine with cumin, salt and pepper and fry for 2 minutes on each side until golden brown. Serve on rocket leaves, squeeze a little lemon juice over the top and serve the fig and redcurrant compote on the side.

Champneys rating

SERVES 10

1 kg/2¼ lb **potatoes**, scrubbed

12 **garlic cloves**, peeled

140 g/5 oz **lamb fillet**

50 g/2 oz **air-dried ham**, thinly sliced

1 tablespoon **extra virgin olive oil**

pinch of **ground cumin**

salt and **pepper**

1 **lemon** and 1 bunch of **rocket leaves**, to serve

fig and redcurrant compote

5 **dried figs**

4 large **shallots**, finely diced

1 tablespoon **clear honey**

2 tablespoons **balsamic vinegar**

90 g/3 oz **redcurrants**

2 teaspoons **wholegrain mustard**

1 sprig **rosemary**

roasted monkfish tail
on a green bean and olive salad

First make the salad; whisk together the lemon juice, vinegar, sugar, mustard, olive oil and a little salt and pepper, then add the herbs and onion. Blanch the beans in salted boiling water for 4 minutes, then drain and refresh in cold water. Drain well, pat dry on kitchen paper and add to the herb dressing, together with the tomatoes. Leave to marinate for 2 hours.

Mix the wine, garlic, lemon zest and juice, sugar, coriander, salt and pepper in a shallow dish, add the monkfish and leave to marinate for 1 hour.

Heat the oven to 230°C/450°F/gas 8. Put the onion wedges in a small roasting tin lined with baking parchment and roast for 15 minutes until tender and browned.

To cook the monkfish, heat a non-stick frying pan over high heat, add the monkfish and turn to seal all over. Continue cooking for 5–6 minutes until golden brown, but still moist in the centre.

While the fish is cooking, strain the bean salad over a jug. Pile the salad in the centre of 4 serving plates. Put the roasted red onion wedges on top and then the monkfish. Add the strained bean salad dressing to the frying pan together with the olives. Warm gently and pour over the fish. Serve warm.

Champneys rating

SERVES 4

3 tablespoons **dry white wine**

1 **garlic clove**, finely chopped

grated zest and juice of 1 **lemon**

1 teaspoon **caster sugar**

1 teaspoon crushed **coriander seeds**

sea salt and freshly ground **black pepper**

1 **monkfish tail** (about 450 g/1 lb), boned and cut into 8 strips

1 **red onion**, cut into 8 wedges

green bean salad

juice of ½ **lemon**

1 tablespoon **white wine vinegar**

1 teaspoon **caster sugar**

1 teaspoon **dijon mustard**

2 tablespoons **extra virgin olive oil**

1 tablespoon chopped **chervil**

1 tablespoon chopped **basil**

1 tablespoon chopped **parsley**

1 tablespoon chopped **fennel herb**

¼ **red onion**, finely chopped

200 g/7 oz **green beans**

3 **tomatoes**, skinned, deseeded and cut into batons

8 **black olives**, pitted and halved

home-smoked sea bass
with sweet and sour cucumber and curly endive

To make the sweet and sour sauce, boil the vinegar, sugar, star anise, garlic, onion and pineapple juice over high heat until the sauce has reduced by three-quarters. Then add the tomato juice and simmer for 4–5 minutes until the sauce is very thick. Strain through a fine sieve and then whisk in the sesame oil, tarragon mustard and sesame seeds.

Run your fingers over the fish and if you feel any small bones, remove them with tweezers. Put the fish into a shallow dish. Mix the salt with 8 tablespoons cold water, then pour over the fish and leave in the brine for 1 hour. Rinse under cold water.

To steam the fish, you will need a wok with a lid and a trivet (or cooling rack) that fits inside the wok and sits about 7 cm/2¾ inches from the base of the wok. Lay the oak twigs and the tarragon in the wok and place the trivet above them. Put a lid on and place the wok over medium heat until the oak twigs begin to smoke. Add the fish, flesh side down, and replace the lid. It will take approximately 15 minutes to smoke the sea bass fillets.

Gently reheat the sauce. Dress the cucumber, curly endive and diced tomatoes in the warm sauce and serve on 4 plates, with a fillet of warm smoked sea bass on top.

Champneys rating

SERVES 4

4 x 90 g/3 oz **sea bass** fillets, skin on

1 tablespoon **salt**

handful of **oak twigs** (it is best if the twigs are fresh from the tree as green oak has a lot of tannin and will give a good flavour)

1 bunch **tarragon**

½ **cucumber**, seeds removed, cut into 2 cm/¾ inch batons

50 g/2 oz **curly endive** (frisée)

2 **tomatoes**, skinned, deseeded and diced

sweet and sour sauce

4 tablespoons **cider vinegar**

2 tablespoons **demerara sugar**

2 **star anise**

1 **garlic clove**, crushed

1 **onion**, chopped

250 ml/8 fl oz **pineapple juice**

6 tablespoons **tomato juice**

1 teaspoon **sesame oil**

1 teaspoon **tarragon mustard**

½ teaspoon **sesame seeds**, toasted

mussels with lemon grass,
spring onions and basil

Rinse the mussels in several changes of clean water, pull out the beards and discard any mussels with broken shells and any that remain open when tapped. Put the shallots, lemon grass, basil stalks, green of spring onions, garlic, lemon zest and vermouth into a large saucepan over high heat. Add the mussels, cover with a tight-fitting lid and steam for about 6 minutes or until the mussels have opened.

Remove from the heat and use a slotted spoon to lift the mussels into a large bowl, discarding any that remain closed; keep warm. Put the cooking liquid back over high heat, whisk in the cornflour mixture and cook for 1 minute. Remove from the heat and whisk in the fromage frais and yoghurt. Liquidize, then pass through a fine sieve into another large pan, add the white of spring onions and the chopped basil, then add the mussels and stir. Serve hot, in deep bowls, garnished with basil sprigs and lime wedges.

Champneys rating

SERVES 4

2 kg/4½ lb **mussels** in their shells, thoroughly scrubbed

8 **shallots**, finely chopped

10 stalks **lemon grass**, finely chopped

1 bunch **basil**, 4 sprigs reserved for garnish, remaining leaves finely chopped, stalks reserved

1 bunch **spring onions**, white parts chopped, green parts reserved

1 **garlic clove**, crushed

grated zest and juice of 1 **lemon**

100 ml/3½ fl oz **dry vermouth**

1 tablespoon **cornflour** dissolved in 1 tablespoon water

2 tablespoons **fromage frais**

1 tablespoon **low-fat yoghurt**

1 **lime**, quartered, to serve

Left: Home smoked sea bass with sweet and sour cucumber

stuffed roasted chillies

with sultana and mint couscous

To make the yoghurt dressing, mix all the ingredients together, then chill in the refrigerator, stirring occasionally to infuse the saffron.

Heat the oven to 190°C/375°F/gas 5. Heat a non-stick frying pan over low heat, add the olive oil, then add the lamb, half the onion and the garlic and fry for 4–5 minutes until golden brown. Add the olives and coriander, squeeze in a little lemon juice and season to taste with salt.

Cut the chillies in half lengthways and, using a teaspoon, gently scrape out the seeds. Stuff the chillies with the minced lamb mixture, then place on a non-stick roasting tin and sprinkle with the grated Parmesan. Roast for 15 minutes.

Mix the soaked sultanas with the couscous and the grated lemon zest. Add the mint, vinegar, sugar and diced tomatoes. Season to taste with salt and pepper.

Serve the roasted chillies on top of the couscous and drizzle the yoghurt around the couscous.

Champneys rating

SERVES 4

½ teaspoon **olive oil**

90 g/3 oz **lamb fillet**, minced

1 **red onion**, chopped

1 **garlic clove**, chopped

6 **green olives**, finely chopped

1 teaspoon chopped **fresh coriander**

grated zest and juice of ½ **lemon**

salt and **pepper**

6 **mild red chillies**

6 **mild green chillies**

25 g/1 oz **parmesan** cheese, grated

25 g/1 oz **sultanas**, soaked in boiling
   water and left to cool

100 g/3½ oz **couscous**, cooked

20 **mint leaves**, shredded

dash of **white wine vinegar**

1 teaspoon **caster sugar**

3 **tomatoes**, skinned, deseeded
   and finely diced

yoghurt dressing

2 tablespoons **low-fat yoghurt**

1 teaspoon **caster sugar**

pinch of **chilli powder**

good pinch of **saffron strands**

bruschetta

with button onions, tomatoes, peppers and parmesan

Put the button onions in a small saucepan. Add the red wine, balsamic vinegar, honey and bay leaves, cover and simmer over low heat until the onions are just tender. Remove the lid, increase the heat and continue to cook until all the liquid has evaporated; this will take about 20 minutes.

Lightly toast the bread on both sides under a low grill so that the bread dries out and becomes crisp. Rub the garlic clove on both sides of the bread.

In a separate saucepan, warm the tomatoes with the pepper and olive oil for 2 minutes. Season to taste with salt and pepper. Add the basil and oregano at the last minute. Pile the onions on to the bread, then add the tomato and pepper mixture and top with shavings of Parmesan. Serve warm.

Champneys rating

SERVES 4

200 g/7 oz **button onions**, peeled

50 ml/2 fl oz **red wine**

2 tablespoons **balsamic vinegar**

1 tablespoon **honey**

3 **bay leaves**

8 thin slices of **crusty bread**

1 **garlic clove**, halved

2 **tomatoes**, skinned, deseeded and roughly chopped

1 **red pepper**, roasted, skinned, deseeded and diced

1 teaspoon **extra virgin olive oil**

salt and **pepper**

1 teaspoon chopped **basil**

½ teaspoon chopped **oregano**

25 g/1 oz **parmesan** cheese, shaved with a potato peeler

roasted scallops

with caramelized chicory and crispy parma ham

Lay the Parma ham on a baking sheet lined with greaseproof paper and place in a very cool oven (100°C/200°F/gas ¼) for 2 hours until dry and crisp. Increase the oven temperature to maximum.

Separate the corals from the scallops. To make the dressing, heat a small non-stick saucepan over medium heat, add the olive oil and garlic and sauté the corals for about 1 minute; the garlic should not colour. Add the vermouth and orange juice and zest and simmer until reduced by half. Then add the passata and bring to the boil. Simmer for 2–3 minutes until it thickens slightly. Liquidize using a hand-held blender and then pass through a fine sieve. Mix in the yoghurt and chopped chives. Season to taste and set aside.

Cut the radicchio and chicory into quarters, leaving the roots on so they do not fall apart. Blanch the radicchio in boiling water, then drain, refresh under cold water and thoroughly squeeze dry on kitchen paper.

Heat a non-stick pan with a metal handle (so that it can be put into a hot oven) over very high heat. Add the grapeseed oil, then add the scallops and brown for 20–30 seconds on each side. Transfer the scallops to a baking sheet and place in the middle of the oven.

Wipe the pan with kitchen paper, add the radicchio and chicory and dry-fry, turning carefully, until browned on all sides. Sprinkle with the sugar and Cointreau and put into the oven, near the top.

After 4 minutes the scallops and chicory will be ready. Serve the scallops on top of the chicory and pour the sauce around the edge. Serve the Parma ham on top and garnish with batons of chives. Serve at once.

Champneys rating

SERVES 4

4 slices of **parma ham**

12 **scallops with corals**

1 tablespoon **olive oil**

1 **garlic clove**, crushed

1 tablespoon **dry vermouth**

finely grated zest and juice of ½ **orange**

2 tablespoons **tomato passata**

1 tablespoon **low-fat yoghurt**

20 **chives**: 15 finely chopped,
    5 cut into 3 cm/1 inch batons

1 small **radicchio**

2 heads of **chicory** (Belgian endive)

1 tablespoon **grapeseed oil**

1 tablespoon **caster sugar**

1 tablespoon **Cointreau**

marinated
sardine fillets
with leeks and red pepper mayonnaise

Blanch the basil in boiling water for 10 seconds and then refresh in ice-cold water. Liquidize the basil thoroughly with 2 tablespoons of the olive oil, then leave to drip through a coffee filter into a clean bowl; do not press or the oil will become cloudy.

Mix the parsley, coriander and oregano with the sugar, wine, lime juice, 1 tablespoon olive oil, salt and pepper in a shallow dish. Take out one-third of the mixture and place in a bowl. Grill the sardine fillets, skin side up, on a non-stick roasting tin for 3 minutes, then put them in the shallow dish with the herb mixture. Steam the leeks for 3 minutes, then put them in the bowl with the herb mixture. Leave the sardines and leeks to marinate in the herb mixture; this could be made a day ahead.

In a food processor, liquidize the potato, red pepper, chilli, olive oil and fromage frais until thick and smooth, like mayonnaise. Season to taste with salt, then pass through a fine sieve.

Serve the sardine fillets and leeks on top of the mayonnaise and squeeze a little lime juice on top. Drizzle the basil oil around the plate.

Champneys rating

SERVES 4

1 small bunch **basil**

3 tablespoons **extra virgin olive oil**

2 tablespoons finely chopped **parsley**

2 tablespoons finely chopped
   coriander

1½ tablespoons finely chopped
   oregano

1 teaspoon **caster sugar**

2 tablespoons **white wine**

juice of 1 **lime** (or 2 if small)

salt and **pepper**

8 **sardines**, filleted

2 small **leeks**, finely sliced

red pepper mayonnaise

1 large **potato**, cooked

1 **red pepper**, roasted, skinned
   and deseeded

½ small **red chilli**, deseeded and
   ground in a mortar and pestle

2 tablespoons **extra virgin olive oil**

1 tablespoon **fromage frais**

grilled lobster tails
with ratatouille, spinach and basil

Heat the oven to 180°C/350°F/gas 4. For the ratatouille, liquidize 1 garlic clove with the white wine, basil, 3 tablespoons water, salt and pepper. Mix with the diced aubergine, place in a roasting tin and cook for 20–25 minutes until soft.

Heat a thick-bottomed saucepan, add 1 tablespoon olive oil, then add the onions and cook over low heat until they caramelize; remove from the pan. Add the remaining olive oil to the pan and heat until smoking. Fry the peppers for 2 minutes until well browned, then remove and add to the onions. Fry the courgettes for 2–3 minutes until well browned, then add to the onions and peppers. Return the onions, peppers and courgettes to the pan, add the cooked aubergine, the remaining garlic clove, passata, balsamic vinegar and honey and cook slowly for 20–30 minutes until it thickens. Add the tomato and parsley to the ratatouille and cook for 4 minutes, then season to taste.

Season the lobster tails with sea salt and black pepper. Heat a non-stick griddle pan over high heat, spray with a little oil and griddle the lobster for 2–3 minutes on each side.

In a saucepan over high heat, wilt the spinach with the basil for 1½ minutes, then remove with a slotted spoon and place in the centre of 4 serving plates; season with salt and pepper. Spoon the ratatouille over the spinach and serve a lobster tail on top of the ratatouille. Squeeze a little lemon juice over the lobster and serve with a little roasted pepper dressing.

Champneys rating

SERVES 4

4 x 100 g/3½ oz raw **lobster tails**, shells removed

sea salt and freshly ground **black pepper**

cooking oil in a spray can

200 g/7 oz **baby spinach**

20 **basil leaves**

½ **lemon**

Roasted red pepper dressing (page 91), to serve

ratatouille

2 **garlic cloves**, finely chopped

100 ml/3½ fl oz **dry white wine**

1 teaspoon chopped **basil**

1 small **aubergine**, cut into 2 cm/ ¾ inch dice

2 tablespoons **extra virgin olive oil**

2 **red onions**, cut into 1 cm/½ inch dice

1 **red**, 1 **green** and 1 **yellow pepper**, cut into 2 cm/¾ inch dice

2 **courgettes**, cut into 2 cm/ ¾ inch dice

6 tablespoons **tomato passata**

1 tablespoon **balsamic vinegar**

1 tablespoon **honey**

6 **tomatoes**, skinned, deseeded and cut into 1 cm/½ inch dice

1 tablespoon chopped **parsley**

venison, leek and apple sausages
with butternut and basil mash

Heat the oven to 240°C/475°F/gas 9. Cut the butternut squash in half and discard the seeds. Roast in the hot oven until cooked, about 25–30 minutes.

In a large bowl, mix the garlic with the mustard, egg, sage, apple and leek. Season to taste with Worcestershire sauce, salt and pepper, then add the minced venison and bacon. Add a few breadcrumbs if the mixture is too wet; you should be able to form it into sausage shapes. Divide the mixture into four, roll into sausage shapes and then roll in cling film and twist the ends. Poach the sausages in the cling film in boiling water for 4 minutes, then leave to cool.

In a small saucepan, boil the chicken stock, balsamic vinegar, ceps and honey over high heat until reduced to a thick syrup, then pass through a fine sieve.

Purée the cooked squash with the basil and fromage frais until smooth. Season to taste with salt and pepper.

Heat a non-stick frying pan and add the olive oil. Remove the cling film from the sausages and fry until lightly browned. Transfer to the hot oven to finish cooking for 8 minutes until golden brown.

Serve the sausages on top of the squash purée and serve the cep sauce around the edge. Garnish with fresh basil leaves.

Champneys rating

SERVES 4

1 **garlic clove**, crushed

1 teaspoon **wholegrain mustard**

1 small **egg**

4 **sage leaves**, finely chopped

1 **cox's apple**, peeled and diced

1 small **leek**, finely chopped

dash of **worcestershire sauce**

salt and **pepper**

100 g/3½ oz **loin of venison**, minced

2 rashers **smoked bacon**, fat removed and minced

2 tablespoons **wholemeal breadcrumbs** (optional)

100 ml/3½ fl oz **chicken stock**

2 tablespoons **balsamic vinegar**

25 g/1 oz **dried ceps** (porcini mushrooms)

1 tablespoon **honey**

2 teaspoons **olive oil**

butternut and basil mash

200 g/7 oz **butternut squash**

10 **basil leaves**, plus extra to garnish

2 tablespoons **fromage frais**

salads and dressings

Salads are a very special feature of the Champneys lunch menu, where salad leaves and vegetables team up with fruit, nuts and seeds – and an utterly delicious range of low-fat and fat-free dressings.

red cabbage salad

with grapes, banana, apple and celery

Put the honey, vinegar, pineapple and orange zest and juice into a thick-bottomed saucepan and bring to the boil. Boil to reduce the liquid by half, then add the red cabbage and cook on a low heat for 8–10 minutes. Leave to cool.

When cool, add the celery, apple, grapes and banana. Mix carefully and then stir in the yoghurt. Season to taste with black pepper and a little salt.

Champneys rating

SERVES 4

1 tablespoon **honey**

2 tablespoons **cider vinegar**

100 g/3½ oz **pineapple**, cut into 1 cm/ ½ inch cubes

finely grated zest and juice of 1 **orange**

200 g/7 oz **red cabbage**, finely shredded

2 sticks **celery**, sliced

1 **green eating apple**, diced

10 **black grapes**, cut in half

1 small **banana**, sliced

3 tablespoons **low-fat yoghurt**

salt and freshly ground **black pepper**

bean salad

with roasted cherry tomatoes and avocado salsa

To make the avocado salsa, mix the coriander seeds with the garlic and most of the chopped coriander (reserving a little for garnish), sugar, lime zest and juice, leek, shallots, chilli and green pepper. Season to taste with a little salt and refrigerate for at least 4 hours.

Heat the oven to 200°C/400°F/gas 6. Put the cherry tomatoes in a small roasting tin and roast for about 10 minutes until they just begin to char and collapse. Leave to cool.

Meanwhile, blanch the runner beans and French beans in boiling water for 1 minute. Drain and refresh in ice-cold water.

Mix all the beans together, mix with the salsa and add the diced avocado. Leave for at least 2 hours to let the flavours develop.

Serve the bean salad on top of the tomatoes and garnish with fresh coriander.

Champneys rating

SERVES 4

20 **cherry tomatoes**

50 g/2 oz **runner beans**, cut into strips

50 g/2 oz **french beans**, cut into 3 cm/1 inch lengths

50 g/2 oz cooked **red kidney beans**

50 g/2 oz cooked **broad beans**, skinned

50 g/2 oz cooked **haricot beans**

avocado salsa

1 teaspoon **coriander seeds**, roasted and crushed

1 **garlic clove**, crushed

1 bunch **coriander**, chopped

1 teaspoon **sugar**

finely grated zest and juice of 4 **limes**

½ **green leek**, finely chopped

4 **shallots**, finely chopped

1 small **green chilli pepper**, finely chopped

1 **green pepper**, cut into 5 mm/ ¼ inch dice

salt

1 **avocado**, cut into 5 mm/¼ inch dice

salad of plums,
peaches, fennel, orange and hazelnuts

Finely grate the zest of the orange, then, using a long sharp knife, cut the fruit into 4 slices, about 1 cm/½ inch thick, holding the orange over a plate to collect the juice. Cut off the orange peel.

To make the dressing, mix the hazelnut oil with the mustard and the juice collected when segmenting the orange. Add the vinegar, sugar, orange zest, lemon zest and juice and liquidize until smooth and frothy.

Pick the heart of the curly endive into small pieces. Mix the plums and peaches with the curly endive, sliced fennel and the chervil leaves. To serve, place a slice of orange on each plate. Dress the salad with the hazelnut dressing, season with black pepper and pile on to the orange slices. Sprinkle with the hazelnuts and serve at once.

Champneys rating

     ♦♦♦

SERVES 4

1 **orange**

1 **curly endive** (frisée)

3 **plums**, quartered

2 **peaches**, cut into 8 wedges

1 small **fennel bulb**, cut into
5 mm/¼ inch slices

1 bunch **chervil**

freshly ground **black pepper**

20 **hazelnuts**, roasted, skins
rubbed off

hazelnut dressing

2 tablespoons **hazelnut oil**

½ teaspoon **tarragon mustard**
or **dijon mustard**

1 teaspoon **tarragon vinegar**
or **white wine vinegar**

1 teaspoon **sugar**

grated zest and juice of ½ **lemon**

fennel, asparagus and walnut salad

with orange mayonnaise

To make the orange mayonnaise, put the potatoes, orange zest and juice, fromage frais, yoghurt and walnut oil in a food processor. Blend until smooth, season to taste with salt and pepper, then pass through a fine sieve.

Steam the fennel for 2 minutes, then set aside. Steam the asparagus for 2 minutes, refresh in ice-cold water, then drain. Pick the heart of the curly endive into small pieces and mix with the walnuts and the herbs. Toss in the orange juice. Pile the leafy salad in the centre of the serving dish and pile the steamed asparagus and fennel on top. Spoon over the orange mayonnaise and grind some Szechwan pepper coarsely over the top.

Champneys rating

SERVES 4

2 **fennel bulbs**, thinly sliced

1 bunch **asparagus**, trimmed and cut into 3 cm/1 inch pieces

1 **curly endive** (frisée)

6 **walnuts**, roasted and chopped into 5 mm/¼ inch pieces

4 tablespoons **chopped mixed herbs** (parsley, chervil, coriander)

juice of 1 **orange**

szechwan peppercorns, in a pepper mill

orange mayonnaise

2 **potatoes**, peeled, diced and cooked until tender

finely grated zest and juice of 2 **oranges**

2 tablespoons **fromage frais**

1 tablespoon **low-fat yoghurt**

2 tablespoons **walnut oil**

salt and **pepper**

salad of tomatoes and quails' eggs

with parmesan crisps

Heat the oven to 190°C/375°F/gas 5. To make the Parmesan crisps, sprinkle the Parmesan in a thin, even layer (less than 1 mm thick) in 8 rough triangular shapes on a non-stick baking sheet. (You can make a template by cutting triangles out of an old plastic lid, using a sharp knife.) Bake for 4–6 minutes until golden brown. When cooked, loosen them carefully with a palette knife and leave to cool on the baking sheet. These crisps can be made in advance and kept in an airtight container until ready to use.

To cook the quails' eggs, carefully break them into gently simmering water to which you have added the vinegar. The eggs will take about 1 minute to cook and should be softly poached. Plunge them into iced water to prevent them from over-cooking.

To make the dressing, liquidize the sun-dried tomatoes with the balsamic vinegar, olive oil, sugar, potato and 4 tablespoons cold water until smooth, then pass through a fine sieve. Season to taste; this dressing will probably not need any salt because of the sun-dried tomatoes, but use lots of black pepper.

To assemble the salad, cut the tomatoes in half and then mix with the salad leaves and drizzle with the dressing. Place in the centre of the serving plates. Drain the poached quails' eggs on kitchen paper and place on the salad. Serve the Parmesan crisps on top.

Champneys rating

SERVES 4

50 g/2 oz **parmesan** cheese, freshly grated

8 fresh **quails' eggs**

1 tablespoon **white wine vinegar**

10 **yellow cherry tomatoes**

10 **red cherry tomatoes**

50 g/2 oz **baby spinach leaves**

50 g/2 oz **baby red chard** or **beetroot leaves**

a few **baby basil leaves**

sun-dried tomato dressing

6 **sun-dried tomatoes**

2 tablespoons **balsamic vinegar**

2 tablespoons **extra virgin olive oil**

½ teaspoon **sugar**

1 small cooked **potato**

salt and freshly ground **black pepper**

curly kale, carrot, celeriac and pink grapefruit salad
with chestnut and mustard dressing

Blanch the curly kale in salted boiling water for 1 minute, then drain and refresh in ice-cold water. Drain the kale on kitchen paper. Peel and segment the grapefruits, holding them over a plate to collect the juice; reserve the juice.

To make the dressing, liquidize the chestnuts with the mustard, oil and the reserved grapefruit juice. Mix the yoghurt and honey into the dressing and season to taste with salt and pepper.

Mix the drained kale with the carrots, celeriac and pink grapefruit segments and then toss the salad with the dressing.

Champneys rating

SERVES 4

100 g/3½ oz **curly kale**

2 **pink grapefruits**

1 large **carrot**, cut into fine strips

50 g/2 oz **celeriac**, cut into fine strips

chestnut and mustard dressing

4 **roasted chestnuts**

1 teaspoon **english mustard**

1 tablespoon **grapeseed oil**

2 tablespoons **low-fat yoghurt**

1 teaspoon **clear honey**

salt and **pepper**

pasta, cauliflower, broccoli and gorgonzola salad

Bring the milk to the boil and then whisk in the dissolved cornflour and cook, stirring, for 1 minute until the milk has the consistency of double cream. Remove from the heat and stir in the gorgonzola and fromage frais, then whisk in the walnut oil and season to taste with black pepper. Cover with cling film to prevent a skin forming and leave to cool.

Cook the pasta in salted boiling water until it is just tender but still firm to the bite (*al dente*). Meanwhile, steam the cauliflower for 1 minute, then refresh in ice-cold water. Steam and refresh the broccoli in the same way. Drain the pasta and mix with the cauliflower, broccoli and leeks.

In a very clean bowl, whisk the egg white until it forms soft peaks. Fold the egg white into the gorgonzola mixture. Fold the pasta and vegetables into the frothy dressing and serve sprinkled with chive batons.

Champneys rating

SERVES 4

50 ml/2 fl oz **skimmed milk**

½ teaspoon **cornflour** dissolved in a little water

25 g/1 oz **gorgonzola** cheese

1 tablespoon **fromage frais**

1 tablespoon **walnut oil**

freshly ground **black pepper**

140 g/5 oz dried **pasta**

100 g/3½ oz small **cauliflower florets**

100 g/3½ oz **broccoli florets**

50 g/2 oz **leeks**, sliced very thinly

1 **egg white**

15 **chives**, cut into 5 cm/2 inch lengths

champneys salade niçoise

To make the dressing, whisk the anchovy essence with the mustard, sugar, vinegar and capers. Finally whisk in the olive oil.

Heat the grill. Cook the swordfish on a non-stick baking sheet under the hot grill for about 5 minutes on each side. Leave to cool in the dressing.

Cook the sugar snap peas in salted boiling water for 1 minute, then drain and refresh in ice-cold water. Blanch the mangetout in salted boiling water, then drain, refresh and cut diagonally. Gently toss the peas and mangetout with all the remaining salad ingredients and serve between layers of swordfish.

Champneys rating

SERVES 4

200 g/7 oz **swordfish**, very thinly sliced

100 g/3½ oz **sugar snap peas**

100 g/3½ oz **mangetout**,

12 **black olives**, halved

1 **red onion**, chopped

2 **beef tomatoes**, skinned, deseeded, and diced

4 **salad potatoes**, cooked and diced

100 g/3½ oz **baby spinach leaves**

1 teaspoon chopped **flat-leaf parsley**

dressing

1 tablespoon **anchovy essence**

½ teaspoon **dijon mustard**

½ teaspoon **sugar**

1 teaspoon **red wine vinegar**

1 teaspoon chopped **capers**

1 tablespoon **extra virgin olive oil**

artichoke, pecan and red chard salad
with maple and lime vinaigrette

Cook the artichokes in salted boiling water for 12–15 minutes, until they are just tender but still firm to the bite – do not over-cook or they will collapse. Drain, then refresh in ice-cold water; drain well.

Cut the cold artichokes into 2 cm/¾ inch dice. Mix the chard and corn salad with the pecan nuts and diced artichokes.

To make the vinaigrette, mix the maple syrup with the mustard, lime zest and juice and the white wine. Then whisk in the oil and season to taste with salt and pepper. Toss the salad in the vinaigrette and leave for 1 hour to let the flavours develop. Serve on ice-cold plates.

Champneys rating

SERVES 4

200 g/7 oz **jerusalem artichokes**,
    washed and scrubbed

100 g/3½ oz **red chard**
    (or **radicchio** or **beetroot leaves**),
    cut into 1 cm/½ inch pieces

25 g/1 oz **corn salad**

50 g/2 oz **pecan nuts**, roughly
    chopped

maple and lime vinaigrette

1 tablespoon **maple syrup**

½ teaspoon **dijon mustard**

finely grated zest and juice of
    1 large **lime**

2 tablespoons **white wine**

1 tablespoon **walnut oil**

1 teaspoon **groundnut oil**

salt and **pepper**

champneys tabbouleh

Put the cracked wheat in a bowl, pour over boiling water to cover and leave the wheat to soak and swell for about 10 minutes.

Mix the mustard, cumin, garlic, lemon zest and juice, olive oil, chopped coriander, mint and parsley together. Then add the remaining ingredients and mix thoroughly with the dressing. Season to taste with salt and pepper, then leave for at least 4 hours before serving; the salad will improve in flavour if made the day before.

Serve at room temperature. Garnish the salad with mint, coriander and parsley.

Champneys rating

♥ ♥

SERVES 4

140 g/5 oz **cracked wheat**

½ teaspoon **dijon mustard**

pinch of **ground cumin**

1 **garlic clove**, crushed

grated zest and juice of 1 **lemon**

2 tablespoons **olive oil**

1 tablespoon chopped **fresh coriander**, plus extra to garnish

2 tablespoons chopped **fresh mint**, plus extra to garnish

3 tablespoons chopped **flat-leaf parsley**, plus extra to garnish

8 cm/3 inch piece of **cucumber**, seeds removed

2 ripe **red tomatoes** and 2 ripe **yellow tomatoes**, skinned, deseeded and cut into 1 cm/½ inch dice

1 **red onion**, finely chopped

salt and freshly ground **black pepper**

fat-free roasted red pepper, chilli and rosemary dressing

SERVES 10–12

1 large **red pepper**

1 **red chilli pepper**, cut in half, deseeded and cored

1 small **potato** (about 25 g/1 oz)

½ clove **garlic**

1 teaspoon **clear honey**

1 tablespoon chopped **rosemary**

1 teaspoon **english mustard**

juice of ½ **lemon**

1 teaspoon **white wine vinegar**

salt and freshly ground **black pepper**

Heat the oven to 230°C/450°F/gas 8. Put the pepper, chilli and potato on a baking sheet and roast in the hot oven until the pepper skin is blackened and the potato is cooked. Halve the pepper over a plate to collect the juice. Pull off the stalk and scrape out the seeds.

Liquidize the pepper with all the remaining ingredients, ideally with a hand-held blender, then pass through a fine sieve. Season to taste with salt and pepper. Keep in the refrigerator for 3–4 days.

Champneys rating

fat-free watercress and rocket dressing with caraway and orange

SERVES 10–12

3 tablespoons roughly torn **rocket leaves**

2 tablespoons **watercress leaves**

finely grated zest and juice of 2 **oranges**

1 small **potato** (about 25 g/1 oz), cooked

1 teaspoon **caraway seeds**, toasted

½ teaspoon **szechwan peppercorns**, crushed

1 tablespoon **clear honey**

2 tablespoons **water**

salt and freshly ground **black pepper**

Blanch the rocket in boiling water for 10 seconds, then drain and refresh in ice-cold water. Blanch the watercress in the same way. This sets the bright green colour of the leaves.

Liquidize all the ingredients, ideally with a hand-held blender, then pass through a fine sieve. Season to taste. Keep in the refrigerator for 3–4 days.

Champneys rating

Dressings, clockwise from top right: Fat-free roasted red pepper, chilli and rosemary; Mango, coconut, lemon grass and lime; Mixed berry, walnut and pink peppercorn; Fat-free watercress and rocket with caraway and orange

ginger, honey and orange dressing

mango, coconut, lemon grass and lime dressing

SERVES 10–12

2 **oranges**

2 tablespoons chopped, peeled **fresh ginger**

3 tablespoons **clear honey**

3 tablespoons **dry white wine**

1 teaspoon **white wine vinegar**

4 tablespoons **water**

1 small **new potato**, cooked

4 tablespoons **grapeseed oil**

2 tablespoons **fromage frais**

1 teaspoon **dijon mustard**

freshly ground **black pepper**

SERVES 10–12

200 g/7 oz over-ripe **mango**, peeled and
   roughly chopped

100 ml/3½ fl oz **coconut milk**

4 stalks **lemon grass**, finely chopped

grated zest and juice of 2 **limes**

4 dried **kaffir lime leaves**

1 teaspoon chopped **coriander**

2 teaspoons **sweet chilli sauce**

2 tablespoons **grapeseed oil**

salt and freshly ground **black pepper**

Grate the zest of the oranges, then cut off the peel and segment the flesh, removing any pips. Put the ginger, honey, wine, vinegar and 4 tablespoons water into a small stainless steel saucepan and bring to the boil. Simmer for 4–5 minutes, then add all the remaining ingredients and liquidize until smooth. Pass through a fine sieve and season to taste with black pepper. Keep in the refrigerator for 3–4 days.

Liquidize all the ingredients until smooth, ideally with a hand-held blender, then pass through a fine sieve. Season to taste with salt and pepper. Keep in the refrigerator for 3–4 days.

Champneys rating

Champneys rating

mixed berry, walnut and pink peppercorn dressing

SERVES 10–12

100 g/3½ oz mixed **red berry fruits**

2 **walnuts**, toasted

12 **pink peppercorns**

½ teaspoon crushed **coriander seeds**

3 teaspoons **walnut oil**

1 teaspoon **sugar**

1 tablespoon **low-fat yoghurt**

1 tablespoon **white wine vinegar**

2 tablespoons **water**

freshly ground **black pepper**

Liquidize all the ingredients until smooth, then pass through a fine sieve. Season to taste with pepper. Keep in the refrigerator for 3–4 days.

Champneys rating

fat-free fresh herb and roasted garlic dressing

SERVES 10–12

3 cloves **garlic**, sliced

1 small **potato** (about 25 g/1 oz), cooked

1 teaspoon crushed **coriander seeds**

1 tablespoon chopped **parsley**

1 tablespoon chopped **coriander**

1 tablespoon chopped **dill**

1 tablespoon chopped **chervil**

1 tablespoon chopped **chives**

3 tablespoons **dry white wine**

1 teaspoon **white wine vinegar**

½ teaspoon **tarragon vinegar**

3 tablespoons **water**

salt and freshly ground **black pepper**

Spread the garlic on a baking sheet and roast under a low grill for 5–6 minutes until lightly browned.

Liquidize all the ingredients, ideally with a hand-held blender, then push through a fine sieve. Season to taste. Keep in the refrigerator for 3–4 days.

Champneys rating

sun-dried tomato, olive and rosemary dressing

SERVES 10–12

50 g/2 oz **sun-dried tomatoes**, soaked in boiling water for 20 minutes, then drained

2 sprigs of **rosemary**, leaves stripped from the stalks

1 small **new potato**, cooked

2 tablespoons pitted and chopped **green olives**

1 **garlic clove**, peeled

3 tablespoons **extra virgin olive oil**

2 tablespoons **balsamic vinegar**

½ teaspoon **dijon mustard**

6 tablespoons **water**

salt and freshly ground **black pepper**

Liquidize all the ingredients until smooth, ideally with a hand-held blender, then pass through a fine sieve and season to taste with salt and pepper. Keep in the refrigerator for 3–4 days.

Champneys rating
♥   🍎

roasted garlic, honey, mustard and lemon dressing

SERVES 10–12

2 whole **garlic bulbs**

1 small **new potato**, cooked

finely grated zest of 1 **lemon**, juice of 2 **lemons**

4 tablespoons **grapeseed oil**

3 tablespoons **clear honey**

2 tablespoons **low-fat yoghurt**

1 tablespoon **white wine vinegar**

6 tablespoons **water**

salt and freshly ground **black pepper**

Heat the oven to 200°C/400°F/gas 6. Peel the garlic, place on a baking sheet and roast for 25 minutes until golden brown.

Liquidize the garlic with all the remaining ingredients, ideally with a hand-held blender, then pass though a fine sieve and season to taste with salt and pepper. Keep in the refrigerator for 3–4 days.

Champneys rating

creamy basil and chive dressing

SERVES 10–12

2 bunches **basil**

4 tablespoons **extra virgin olive oil**

6 tablespoons **fromage frais**

½ bunch **chives**

1 tablespoon **white wine vinegar**

¼ tablespoon **english mustard powder**

1 tablespoon **clear honey**

salt and freshly ground **black pepper**

Blanch the basil in boiling water for 10 seconds, then drain and refresh in ice-cold water. This sets the deep green colour of the leaves.

Liquidize all the ingredients, ideally with a hand-held blender. Leave for 1 hour to allow the flavours to develop and improve, then pass through a fine sieve and season to taste with salt and pepper. Keep in the refrigerator for 3–4 days.

Champneys rating

main courses

Lunch or dinner can be adventurous as well as healthy, pleasing the senses with exciting combinations of flavours, colours and textures, and satisfying the body with the nutrients it needs.

crispy polenta
layered with mushrooms and rocket pesto

Bring 250 ml/8 fl oz water to the boil in a saucepan, add a good pinch of salt, then whisk in the polenta, bring back to the boil and cook, stirring constantly, for 5 minutes. Pour the polenta on to a baking sheet (about 30 x 25 cm/12 x 10 inches) to form a thin layer, about 5 mm/¼ inch thick. Alternatively, pour the polenta into a small terrine or loaf tin. Put the polenta in the refrigerator until cold and firm. Cut the polenta into squares (about 8 x 8 cm/3 x 3 inches) or turn out of the tin and cut into 12–16 very thin slices – the thinner the better. Lay the slices on a large baking sheet lined with greaseproof paper, then dry out very slowly in the oven at its lowest setting; this will take several hours. When the polenta is crisp, remove from the oven and set aside.

To make the pesto, heat the olive oil in a saucepan and sweat the rocket until wilted, then leave to cool. Using a hand-held blender or a mortar and pestle, blend the rocket with the pine nuts, Parmesan, basil and parsley. Season to taste with black pepper and a little lemon juice.

Put the mushrooms in a large saucepan with the red wine, coriander seeds, garlic and sugar and simmer gently until the liquid has reduced to a few tablespoons. Season to taste with salt and pepper. Add the leek and peppers and cook for another 10 minutes until the leek is soft. Remove from the heat and stir in the tarragon, parsley and fromage frais and check the seasoning.

To serve, spread a little of the pesto on the crisp polenta and layer the mushroom mixture between the polenta slices.

Champneys rating

SERVES 4

200 g/7 oz quick-cooking **polenta**

salt and freshly ground black **pepper**

200 g/7 oz mixed **mushrooms**

200 ml/7 fl oz **red wine**

1 teaspoon **coriander seeds**, crushed

1 tablespoon chopped **garlic**

2 teaspoons **sugar**

1 **leek**, cut into 1 cm/½ inch pieces

2 **red peppers**, roasted, skinned and cut into 1 cm/½ inch pieces

1 tablespoon chopped **tarragon**

1 tablespoon chopped **parsley**

1 tablespoon **fromage frais**

rocket pesto

2 tablespoons **extra virgin olive oil**

50 g/2 oz **rocket** leaves

40 g/1½ oz **pine nuts**, toasted

25 g/1 oz **parmesan** cheese, grated

1 tablespoon chopped **basil** leaves

1 tablespoon chopped **parsley**

juice of ¼ **lemon**

refried bean and avocado cakes

with avocado and corn salsa

Drain the beans and pat dry with kitchen paper. Mash the beans to a paste with a potato masher. With a pestle and mortar, crush the fresh chilli with the roasted garlic, coriander seeds and cumin. Add the juice of 1 lime and mix with the beans. Add the grated cheese, shallots and diced avocado and mix carefully so that you do not crush the avocado. Season to taste with salt and pepper. Divide the mixture into 8 balls, then, using your hands, form into cakes approximately 1 cm/½ inch thick. Place on a baking sheet lined with baking parchment and refrigerate until ready to cook.

To make the salsa, toast the sweetcorn in a non-stick pan over a high heat. It is important that you keep stirring so that the sweetcorn colours evenly. When the sweetcorn is toasted, mix with the onion, tomato, sweet chilli sauce and coriander. Finally, stir in the avocado and lime juice and season to taste with a little salt.

To serve, heat the oven to 200°C/400°F/gas 6. Bake the bean cakes for approximately 15 minutes, turning after 7 minutes, until they are evenly coloured.

Serve the hot bean cakes on the cold salsa, add a little low-fat crème fraîche and a lime quarter and serve at once.

Champneys rating

SERVES 4

200 g/7 oz **red kidney beans**, soaked overnight and cooked until tender

1 **red chilli**, deseeded and chopped

4 **garlic cloves**, roasted

pinch of crushed, roasted **coriander seeds**

pinch of **ground cumin**

juice of 1 **lime**, plus 1 **lime**, quartered, to serve

50 g/2 oz **low-fat cheddar cheese**, grated

6 **shallots**, finely chopped

½ **avocado**, finely diced

sea salt and **pepper**

2 tablespoons **low-fat crème fraîche**

avocado and corn salsa

50 g/2 oz frozen **sweetcorn kernels**, thawed

1 small **onion**, chopped

1 **tomato**, skinned, deseeded and diced

2 teaspoons **sweet chilli sauce**

1 bunch **coriander**, leaves roughly torn

½ **avocado**, diced

juice of 2 **limes**

butternut squash and onion tartlets
with apples and pesto

Heat the oven to 220°C/425°F/gas 7. Lay one sheet of filo pastry on a work surface and brush with egg white. Place another sheet of pastry, brushed with egg white on both sides, on top. Cut the pastry in half and place in 2 individual fluted flan tins. Repeat, using the remaining filo pastry to line another 2 flan tins. Bake for 8 minutes or until golden brown. These can be made in advance and kept in an airtight container.

To make the pesto, using a liquidizer or pestle and mortar, blend the basil, garlic, pine nuts, olive oil and Parmesan to a smooth paste. (Alternatively you could buy a jar of pesto.)

Cut the apples into large wedges and place in a bowl of water with the lemon juice to prevent browning. Put two non-stick baking sheets in the oven to heat. Toss the butternut squash with most of the pesto and roast on one of the baking sheets for about 20 minutes. Place the onions on the second baking sheet and drizzle with a little olive oil. Roast for 10–15 minutes.

In a small saucepan, boil the balsamic vinegar and sugar over a high heat to form a caramel, then leave to cool.

Mix the remaining pesto with the drained apple wedges and warm gently under the grill; do not cook the apple. When the squash is tender and browned, spoon it into the warmed filo pastry cases, along with the roasted onions, the warmed apple and a few basil leaves. Spoon the diced tomato and a little of the balsamic mixture around the tartlets and serve at once, with a bitter leaf salad.

Champneys rating

SERVES 4

4 sheets **filo pastry**

1 **egg white**, lightly beaten

2 **red eating apples**

2 **green eating apples**

juice of 1 **lemon**

1 large **butternut squash**, peeled
and cut into 2 cm/¾ inch wedges

6 **red onions**, each cut into 6 wedges

a little **olive oil**

3 tablespoons **balsamic vinegar**

1 tablespoon **sugar**

½ bunch **basil**

1 **tomato**, skinned, deseeded
and diced

pesto

1 bunch **basil**, leaves roughly torn

1 **garlic clove**, chopped

2 tablespoons **pine nuts**, roasted

2 tablespoons **extra virgin olive oil**

2 tablespoons freshly grated
parmesan cheese

filo layers with caramelized shallots
roasted carrots, cashews and broccoli

Heat the oven to 190°C/375°F/gas 5. Lay one sheet of filo pastry on a work surface and brush very lightly with melted olive oil spread. Put another sheet of pastry on top and brush with more olive oil spread. Using a 7 cm/2¾ inch cutter, cut out 8 filo pastry discs. Repeat with the other two sheets of pastry. Place on a non-stick baking sheet and bake for 6−7 minutes or until golden brown. These can be made in advance and kept in an airtight container.

Heat the oven to 220°C/425°F/gas 7. Roast the carrots with ½ teaspoon of the sesame oil, turning often until they are cooked and evenly browned. This will take 15−20 minutes.

In a non-stick frying pan over a moderate heat, gently sweat the shallots in ½ teaspoon of the sesame oil, stirring often until they are evenly golden brown.

To make the sauce, mix the coconut milk with the lime juice and zest, peanut butter, tahini, chilli powder and lemon grass to make a thick paste. Place over a very low heat to allow the lemon grass to infuse for at least 15 minutes. Do not boil.

Heat a non-stick frying pan or wok over a high heat. Stir-fry the broccoli in the remaining sesame oil with the chilli and garlic for about 1 minute, then add the soy sauce and 2 tablespoons water and stir to mix. Add the spinach, cashews, roasted carrots and shallots and stir together.

Add the herbs and yoghurt to the coconut and lemon grass infusion and liquidize until smooth, then pass through a fine sieve. Warm the filo discs in the oven for 1 minute. To serve, layer the filo discs with the stir-fried vegetables, finishing with a layer of filo. Spoon a little of the sauce around the outside and serve at once.

SERVES 4

4 sheets **filo pastry**

2 teaspoons **olive oil spread**, melted

2 large **carrots**, cut into 3 cm/ 1 inch batons

2 teaspoons **dark sesame oil**

16 **shallots**, peeled and sliced

1 large head of **broccoli**, cut into very small florets

1 **red chilli**, finely chopped

1 **garlic clove**, finely chopped

1 teaspoon **soy sauce**

100 g/3½ oz **baby spinach**

2 tablespoons chopped **unsalted cashew nuts**

peanut and coconut sauce

3 tablespoons **coconut milk**

grated zest and juice of 1 **lime**

1 tablespoon **peanut butter**

1 teaspoon **tahini**

pinch of **chilli powder**

3 **lemon grass** stalks, finely chopped

1 tablespoon chopped **mint**

1 tablespoon chopped **coriander**

1 teaspoon chopped **basil**

2 tablespoons **low-fat yoghurt**

Champneys rating

grilled aubergine parcels

with goats' cheese, tomatoes, olives and basil

Slice the aubergines lengthways as thinly as possible with a very sharp knife or a mandolin slicer. You will need 4 slices per person. Cook the aubergines in a large saucepan of salted boiling water for 2 minutes, then refresh and drain on kitchen paper.

Put the onion and chopped garlic into a saucepan and then strain the juice of the tomatoes on top. Cook over a high heat until reduced by two-thirds. Then add the chopped tomatoes, reduce the heat slightly and continue cooking for about 5 minutes or until the mixture is quite dry. Leave to cool.

Lay a slice of aubergine on a chopping board and then lay another slice across the centre to make a cross shape. Put a piece of goats' cheese in the centre of the aubergine cross, then add a little of the tomato and onion mixture, a couple of fresh basil leaves and then 2 olives and a little more tomato mixture and basil. Fold the aubergine ends in to the centre to form a parcel. Repeat with the remaining aubergine slices until you have 8 parcels.

Heat the oven to 220°C/425°F/gas 7. Heat a griddle pan over a high heat. Mix 1 tablespoon of olive oil with the lemon juice, salt and pepper; brush this mixture over the aubergine parcels. Cook the parcels on the griddle pan for 1 minute on each side, then place in the oven for 6–8 minutes. Put the whole cherry tomatoes, the sliced shallots and sliced garlic in a small roasting tin with 1 tablespoon olive oil and roast for 5 minutes.

Serve 2 aubergine parcels per person, with a spoonful of the roasted cherry tomato and shallot mixture, a few pine nuts and a few sprigs of basil.

Champneys rating

SERVES 4

2 large **aubergines**, topped and tailed

1 large **onion**, chopped

4 **garlic cloves**: 2 finely chopped, 2 sliced

200 g/7 oz canned chopped **tomatoes**

100 g/3½ oz soft **goats' cheese**, kept in the freezer for 15–20 minutes to make it easier to cut, then sliced into 8

1 bunch **basil**

16 **black olives**, pitted

2 tablespoons **olive oil**

juice of 1 **lemon**

sea salt and freshly ground **black pepper**

140 g/5 oz **cherry tomatoes**, red and yellow

4 **shallots**, sliced

25 g/1 oz **pine nuts**, toasted

grilled pepper risotto
with fresh herbs

Cut the peppers in half and then into quarters lengthways. Remove the stalks and seeds and cook under a hot grill until the skins have blistered and blackened in places. Put the peppers in a dish, cover and leave until they are cool enough to handle and the skin can be easily peeled off.

Meanwhile, heat a non-stick saucepan over a low heat, add the onions, cover with a lid and cook until translucent, about 2 minutes. Bring the stock to simmering point.

Add the rice to the onions and stir to mix. Drain the ceps, reserving their soaking liquid. Add the ceps to the rice, then slowly pour in the liquid, being careful not to add any grit or sediment from the bottom. Add the hot vegetable stock a little at a time, stirring frequently to prevent the rice from sticking. Add the stock gradually; bring to the boil and let the rice absorb the liquid before adding more. This will take 15–20 minutes.

To serve, stir in the wine, Parmesan and crème fraîche, then stir in half of the chopped herbs. Serve the grilled peppers on top of the rice, garnish with the remaining herbs and serve at once.

SERVES 4

3 **peppers**

2 **onions**, finely chopped

1 litre/1¾ pints **vegetable stock**

100 g/3½ oz **arborio rice**

40 g/1½ oz **dried ceps** (porcini mushrooms), soaked in hot water to cover

1 glass **dry white wine**

1 tablespoon freshly grated **parmesan** cheese

2 tablespoons **low-fat crème fraîche**

2 sprigs **tarragon**, chopped

2 sprigs **chervil**, chopped

1 bunch **chives**, chopped

4 sprigs **basil**

Champneys rating

salmon with sun-dried tomato rosti

with prawn and red pepper salsa

First make the rosti. Heat the oven to 220°C/425°F/gas 7. Coarsely grate the potatoes into a large bowl, stir in the sun-dried tomatoes and season with black pepper. Heat 4 rosti pans, add 1 teaspoon of olive oil to each pan and divide the potato mixture between the rosti pans. (Alternatively, line a baking sheet with baking parchment and divide the potato mixture between four 7 cm/2¾ inch diameter metal pastry cutters.) Press the mixture down with a spoon and bake in the hot oven for 15 minutes.

To make the salsa, liquidize 2 of the roasted peppers with the balsamic vinegar, olive oil, chilli and lime juice. Chop the remaining pepper into small dice. Pour the liquidized pepper mixture into a small saucepan and add the diced pepper, prawns, shallots and parsley; season to taste and set aside.

Heat a non-stick frying pan with a metal handle and fry the mushrooms and garlic in the walnut oil over a high heat. When the mushrooms are tender, remove from the heat and season with a little salt and pepper. Remove from the pan and keep warm.

Reheat the pan and seal the salmon portions on the flesh side, then turn and cook the skin side for a minute or two. Put the pan in the hot oven for 6–8 minutes to finish cooking the salmon.

To serve, gently warm the salsa, but do not boil. Mix the tarragon with the warm mushrooms and then spoon them around the edge of 4 serving plates. Turn out the rosti on to the plates, put the salmon on top and spoon a little salsa over the salmon.

Champneys rating

SERVES 4

200 g/7 oz **oyster mushrooms**

1 **garlic clove**, crushed

1 teaspoon **walnut oil**

salt and freshly ground **black pepper**

4 x 120 g/4 oz **salmon** portions, scaled, skin left on

1 sprig **tarragon**, chopped

sun-dried tomato rosti

500 g/1 lb 2 oz **potatoes**, peeled and par-boiled for 3–5 minutes so that the potato is undercooked

25 g/1 oz **sun-dried tomatoes**, soaked in warm water, then finely chopped

4 teaspoons **extra virgin olive oil**

prawn and red pepper salsa

3 small **red peppers**, roasted

1 teaspoon **balsamic vinegar**

2 tablespoons **extra virgin olive oil**

½ **red chilli**, finely chopped

juice of 1 **lime**

100 g/3½ oz fresh peeled **prawns**

2 small **shallots**, finely chopped

1 tablespoon chopped **parsley**

blackened snapper
with seafood gumbo

Skin the fish fillets and run your fingers over the fish to check that all the bones have been removed; pull out any remaining small bones with tweezers. Mix together the cayenne, dried oregano and thyme, onion powder, paprika, black pepper, salt and lime zest and rub on both sides of the red snapper fillets. Set aside.

To make the seafood gumbo, heat a large, thick-bottomed saucepan, add the oil and sweat the aubergine, pepper, onion, celery and garlic until limp. Add the rice, kidney beans, okra, bay leaves, thyme, cayenne, paprika, lemon zest and juice, passata and stock. Bring to the boil and cook for 20–30 minutes until the rice is nearly cooked.

Meanwhile, scrub the mussels and debeard them, discarding any mussels that are broken or that remain open when tapped firmly. Peel and devein the prawns and roughly chop. Add the mussels and prawns to the gumbo, remove from the heat and stir in the crab meat. Cover with the lid and set aside, stirring occasionally.

Heat a non-stick griddle pan over a high heat and cook the red snapper fillets for 3 minutes on each side until blackened. Remove the bay leaves and thyme from the gumbo and stir in the tomatoes and parsley. Serve the red snapper on top of the gumbo; squeeze on some fresh lime juice and garnish with oregano.

Champneys rating

SERVES 4

4 **red snapper** fillets (about 90 g/ 3 oz each)

½ teaspoon each of **cayenne pepper, dried oregano, dried thyme, onion powder**

¼ teaspoon each of **paprika** and ground **black pepper,** pinch of **salt**

grated zest and juice of 1 **lime**

seafood gumbo

1 teaspoon **grapeseed oil**

1 small **aubergine**, 1 **green pepper,** 1 **onion**, 1 stick **celery**, diced

2 **garlic cloves**, crushed

50 g/2 oz **brown rice**

25 g/1 oz cooked **kidney beans**

8 **okra**, cut in half

3 **bay leaves** and 2 sprigs **thyme**

pinch each of **cayenne** and **paprika**

grated zest and juice of 1 **lemon**

125 ml/4 fl oz **tomato passata**

500 ml/16 fl oz **fish stock**

8–10 **mussels** in shells

4 **tiger prawns**

2 tablespoons **brown crab meat**

2 **tomatoes**, skinned, deseeded and diced

2 tablespoons chopped **parsley**

fresh **oregano**, to garnish

red mullet with spiced gazpacho
cracked wheat with olives and anchovies

Cook the cracked wheat in salted boiling water for 5 minutes, then drain, refresh under cold running water and drain thoroughly, squeezing out all excess water. Mix the olives with the anchovies and paprika. Add the cracked wheat and mix thoroughly. This is best prepared 2–3 hours in advance so that the flavours mingle.

Heat the oven to 140°C/275°F/gas 1. Run your fingers over the fish to check that all the bones have been removed; pull out any remaining small bones with tweezers.

Mix the lemon zest and juice, paprika, cayenne, cumin, saffron, sugar, olive oil, garlic, sherry vinegar, tomato purée and passata, wine and a little salt and pepper. Then add the chopped peppers and onion and mix thoroughly. Spoon a little of the mixture into a casserole dish with a lid, lay the red mullet fillets on top and then cover the fillets with the remaining mixture. Put the lid on and cook in the oven for 30 minutes. When cooked, carefully remove the red mullet fillets from the sauce. Keep warm.

Strain the sauce through a fine sieve into a saucepan. Boil the liquid to reduce by half and keep the strained vegetables warm. Then return the vegetables to the liquid and add the chopped tomatoes. Warm the cracked wheat and serve on 4 warmed plates. Serve the red mullet on top of the cracked wheat and spoon the sauce on top.

Champneys rating

SERVES 4

4 **red mullet** (about 450 g/1 lb in total), filleted

grated zest and juice of 1 **lemon**

pinch each of **paprika**, **cayenne pepper**, **ground cumin**, **saffron strands**

1 tablespoon **sugar**

2 tablespoons **extra virgin olive oil**

2 **garlic cloves**, finely chopped

2 teaspoons **sherry vinegar**

1 tablespoon **tomato purée**

200 ml/7 fl oz **tomato passata**

3 tablespoons **dry white wine**

salt and **pepper**

1 **red**, 1 **green** and 1 **yellow pepper**, finely chopped

1 large **onion**, finely chopped

6 **tomatoes**, skinned, deseeded and chopped

cracked wheat with olives and anchovies

200 g/7 oz **cracked wheat**

10 **black olives**, pitted and chopped

4 canned **anchovy fillets**, chopped

1 teaspoon **smoked paprika** (or regular paprika)

hake with mussels
lemon grass and coconut

In a large, thick-bottomed saucepan over a high heat, dry-fry the onion, carrots, celery and leeks, stirring continuously for 2 minutes. Add the bay leaves, coriander, lemon grass, garlic and lemon zest, then add the mussels, stir and then add the vermouth. Cover with a tight-fitting lid and continue cooking over a high heat for 4–5 minutes, stirring occasionally until the mussels open. Strain into a colander over a clean saucepan to collect the cooking liquid. Cover the colander of mussels, discarding the bay leaves and any mussels that have not opened.

Heat a non-stick frying pan until very hot. Add the oil and then the fish fillets. Cook for 3–4 minutes on each side. (If you have a non-stick pan with a metal handle, put the pan into a very hot oven for 6 minutes. This will roast the hake fillets to perfection.)

Bring the mussel cooking liquid back to the boil. Boil until reduced by half, then add the lemon juice and coconut milk. Return to the boil and whisk in the arrowroot to thicken the sauce. Remove from the heat and stir in the crème fraîche and chives, then return the mussels and vegetables to the pan and stir to mix. To serve, pile the mussels into serving dishes and place the hake fillets on top.

Champneys rating

SERVES 4

1 large **onion**, finely chopped

2 **carrots**, cut into fine strips

2 sticks **celery**, cut into fine strips

2 **leeks**, cut into 5 cm/2 inch pieces, then into fine strips

4 **bay leaves**

1 teaspoon crushed **coriander seeds**

6 large **lemon grass** stalks, chopped

2 **garlic cloves**, crushed

grated zest and juice of 1 **lemon**

500 g/1 lb 2 oz **mussels** in shells, thoroughly scrubbed and debearded

50 ml/2 fl oz **dry vermouth**

1 teaspoon **grapeseed oil**

4 **hake** fillets (about 100 g/3½ oz each), skinned and boned

100 ml/3½ fl oz **coconut milk**

1 teaspoon **arrowroot** mixed with a little water

1 teaspoon **low-fat crème fraîche**

1 bunch **chives**, chopped

salmon with leek fondue

and roasted truffle potatoes

Heat the oven to 220°C/425°F/gas 7. Scrub the potatoes, cut into quarters and place in a roasting tin. Sprinkle with a little truffle oil and lemon thyme and roast for 20 minutes.

Cut the leeks into 3 cm/1 inch chunks (there should be about 20 chunks) and keep the outer leaves as you'll need them to make the sauce. Place the leeks in an ovenproof dish with the garlic, bay leaf and a little lemon thyme. Add the olive oil and wine, cover with a lid and bake for 40 minutes or until the leeks are very soft.

To make the sauce, finely chop the leek trimmings and place in a small saucepan. Add just enough boiling water to cover, then simmer on a low heat for 5 minutes or until soft and tender. Blanch the basil in boiling water for 10 seconds, then drain and refresh under cold running water and chop finely. Drain the liquid from the cooked leeks and add to the leek trimmings, together with the sherry vinegar, crème fraîche and basil. Season to taste with salt and pepper, then pass the sauce through a very fine sieve.

Heat a large non-stick frying pan, add the salmon (but no oil) and fry over a moderate heat for 6–7 minutes until cooked. To serve, place the roasted potatoes and leek fondue in the centre of 4 serving plates and top with the salmon. Drizzle the leek sauce around the plate.

Champneys rating

SERVES 4

250 g/9 oz **red-skinned potatoes**

a little **truffle oil**

1 bunch **lemon thyme**

4 thin **leeks**

3 **garlic cloves**, thinly sliced

1 **bay leaf**

1 teaspoon **olive oil**

½ glass **dry white wine**

1 bunch **basil**

1 teaspoon **sherry vinegar**

2 tablespoons **low-fat crème fraîche**

salt and **pepper**

4 × 100 g/3½ oz **salmon** portions, skin and bones removed

hot smoked salmon

with grilled artichokes
and wasabi mayonnaise

Run your fingers over the salmon to check that all the bones have been removed; pull out any remaining small bones with tweezers. Dissolve the salt in 125 ml/4 fl oz cold water and pour over the salmon pieces in a shallow dish. Leave in the brine for 1½ hours.

To prepare the artichokes, trim the stalks, pull off the outer leaves and cut off the tops using a long sharp knife, rubbing the cut surfaces with a lemon half to prevent discoloration. Cut each artichoke in half, then cook in salted boiling water, to which you have added the squeezed juice and shell of the remaining lemon half. Boil for 15 minutes, then drain and refresh in cold water. Drain well.

To smoke the fish, you will need a wok with a lid and a trivet (or cooling rack) that fits inside the wok and sits about 7 cm/2¾ inches above the base of the wok. Lay the oak twigs and fennel seeds in the bottom, then place the trivet in the wok. Rinse the fish in cold water and lay on the trivet, cover with a lid and put the wok on a low heat for 20 minutes until the fish has hot smoked; it should still be pink in the centre. Leave the fish in the wok.

Make the wasabi mayonnaise by mixing all the ingredients together. Set aside.

Heat a griddle pan over a medium heat. Mix half the olive oil with the chilli, sugar, lemon zest and juice and soy sauce; brush over the artichokes. Cook on the griddle pan for 2 minutes on each side. Heat the remaining olive oil in a saucepan, add the basil and cook over medium–high heat, stirring frequently, for about 30 seconds. Serve at once with the grilled artichokes, warm smoked salmon and wasabi mayonnaise.

SERVES 4

4 centre cut **salmon fillet** pieces
  (120 g/4 oz each), skinned

1 tablespoon **sea salt**

12 **baby globe artichokes**

1 **lemon**, halved

handful of **oak twigs** (see page 66)

3 tablespoons **fennel seeds**

2 tablespoons **olive oil**

1 small **red chilli**, finely chopped

1 teaspoon **sugar**

grated zest and juice of 1 **lemon**

dash of **dark soy sauce**

large handful of **basil** leaves

wasabi mayonnaise

2 tablespoons **low-fat mayonnaise**

½ teaspoon **wasabi paste**

juice of ½ **lime**

1 teaspoon **honey**

Champneys rating

piri piri john dory
with polenta chips

First, make the ketchup. Heat the oven to 200°C/400°F/gas 6. Put the halved tomatoes in a roasting tin and sprinkle over the garlic, sugar, cumin, thyme, spice and balsamic vinegar. Roast for 15–20 minutes until the tomatoes are soft. Put the roasted tomatoes in a blender, add the tomato purée and mustard and blend until smooth. Pass through a sieve and season to taste with salt and pepper.

To make the polenta chips, bring 800 ml/1¼ pints water to the boil in a saucepan. Season with dried oregano, salt and pepper and gently whisk in the polenta. Bring back to the boil, then cook on a low heat for 5 minutes, stirring occasionally. Pour the hot polenta on to a non-stick baking sheet in a 5 mm/¼ inch thick layer and leave to cool. Heat the oven to 200°C/400°F/gas 6. When the polenta is cool, turn out on to a chopping board and cut into 4 cm x 5 mm/1½ x ¼ inch 'chips'. Return to the baking sheet, spray with a little oil and bake in the oven for 15–20 minutes until crisp and golden brown.

Lightly dust the John Dory fillets with piri piri mix and salt. In a non-stick frying pan, heat the oil until smoking and then fry the fish for 3–4 minutes or until cooked, turning once.

To serve, stack the polenta chips on 4 serving plates and put the fish on top. Squeeze a little lime juice over the fish. Serve with the tomato ketchup and a lime wedge.

Champneys rating

SERVES 4

4 **John Dory** fillets (140 g/5 oz each)

2 teaspoons **piri piri** mix

salt and **pepper**

1 tablespoon **grapeseed oil**

2 **limes**, cut into wedges

tomato ketchup

6 **tomatoes**, halved and deseeded

1 **garlic clove**, sliced

40 g/1½ oz sugar

pinch each of **ground cumin**, **dried thyme** and **mixed spice**

3 tablespoons **balsamic vinegar**

1 teaspoon **tomato purée**

1 teaspoon **dijon mustard**

polenta chips

1 teaspoon dried **oregano**

200 g/7 oz quick-cooking **polenta**

sunflower oil in a spray can

sea bass with crab
smoked salmon, cucumber and tarragon salsa

To make the salsa, mix the vinegar with the sugar and mustard. Add the olive oil, tarragon, cucumber, smoked salmon, onion and tomatoes. Season to taste with salt and pepper and leave in the refrigerator for at least 1 hour.

Heat the oven to 200°C/400°F/gas 6. Run your fingers over the fish to check that all the bones have been removed; pull out any remaining small bones with tweezers. Mix the crab meat with the breadcrumbs, chives and egg and season to taste. Spread half the mixture on to 4 of the pieces of sea bass. Place the other pieces of fish on top and spread with the remaining crab mixture. Place on a non-stick baking sheet and cook in the oven for 15–18 minutes.

Heat a large thick-bottomed saucepan over a high heat. Add the olive oil and spinach and cover with a lid. Cook for 1–2 minutes, stirring regularly, until the spinach is cooked. Season with salt and pepper and then drain in a colander. Serve on 4 warmed plates and place the fish on top of the spinach. Serve a little salsa around the outside and squeeze the lemon juice over the fish.

Champneys rating

SERVES 4

4 **sea bass** fillets (100 g/3½ oz each), skinned, cut in half

50 g/2 oz **white crab meat**

2 tablespoons **wholemeal breadcrumbs**

1 bunch **chives**, chopped

1 small **egg**, beaten

salt and freshly ground **black pepper**

1 tablespoon **olive oil**

500 g/1 lb 2 oz **baby spinach**, washed

1 **lemon**, halved

smoked salmon, cucumber and tarragon salsa

2 tablespoons **tarragon white wine vinegar**

1 tablespoon **sugar**

1 teaspoon **dijon mustard**

1 tablespoon **olive oil**

4 sprigs **tarragon**, chopped

100 g/3½ oz **cucumber**, seeds removed, diced

40 g/1½ oz **smoked salmon**, diced

1 small **red onion**, diced

2 **tomatoes**, skinned, deseeded and diced

salt cod with sweet pepper, tomato and olive sauce

with mustard mashed potato

The salt cod must be prepared at least 24 hours ahead. Put the cod in a bowl under cold running water for 1 hour. Then leave it to soak in a large container of cold water for at least 24 hours, changing the water as often as possible. This will rehydrate the cod; you will then be able to skin the fish and cut it into 4 pieces.

To make the sauce, heat a thick-bottomed saucepan, add the olive oil and cook the onion, celery and fennel over a very low heat with the star anise until the vegetables are soft and caramelized; this will take about 30 minutes.

Meanwhile, for the mustard mashed potato, boil the potatoes in salted water until soft. Drain and keep warm.

Add the wine to the caramelized vegetables and boil to reduce by two-thirds, then add the peppers, tomatoes, anchovies and olives and simmer for 10 minutes.

Heat the oven to 200°C/400°F/gas 6. Put the finely chopped onion in an ovenproof dish, lay the soaked cod on top, season with black pepper and add the vermouth. Cover with a lid and place in the oven for 15 minutes until the fish is tender.

To the cooked potatoes, add the capers, mustard and fromage frais and mash until smooth. When the fish is cooked, lift it out of the dish and keep warm. Strain the onions, adding the liquid to the sauce and the onions to the mashed potato. Check the sauce for seasoning. Serve the fish on top of the mash and spoon the sauce over the fish. Garnish with parsley.

Champneys rating

SERVES 4

350 g/13 oz **salt cod**

1 **onion**, finely chopped

freshly ground **black pepper**

2 tablespoons **dry vermouth**

flat-leaf **parsley**, to garnish

sweet pepper, tomato and olive sauce

2 tablespoons **olive oil**

1 **onion**, roughly chopped

4 sticks **celery**, destringed and roughly chopped

1 **fennel bulb**, cut into 8 wedges

4 **star anise**

100 ml/3½ fl oz **dry white wine**

4 **red peppers**, roasted, skinned, deseeded and diced

6 **plum tomatoes**, skinned, deseeded and cut into large dice

3 canned **anchovy fillets**, chopped

8 **black** and 8 **green olives**, pitted

mustard mashed potato

400 g/14 oz **potatoes**, peeled

2 tablespoons **capers**, rinsed in cold water, chopped

1 tablespoon **wholegrain mustard**

2 tablespoons **fromage frais**

warm skate and potato terrine

with rocket salad

This terrine must be prepared in advance, ideally a day ahead, because it needs to be pressed.

Heat the oven to 190°C/375°F/gas 5. Wrap the skate wings in foil, place on a baking sheet and cook in the oven for 15 minutes. Boil the potatoes until they are well cooked; this will enable you to achieve a more compact terrine. Line a small terrine dish or loaf tin with cling film, leaving it overhanging at the sides.

When the skate is cooked, carefully remove the flesh and discard the bones. Layer the warm potato and warm skate in the terrine, seasoning the layers and making sure that you do not leave any gaps between the layers. When the potato is 1 cm/½ inch above the top of the terrine, fold the overhanging cling film over the top and put a very heavy weight on top. Leave until cold, then place in the refrigerator for at least 4 hours or overnight.

In a liquidizer, blend the avocado, lemon juice and chilli powder until smooth.

Remove the terrine from the refrigerator and gently ease out, using the cling film; leave the cling film in place so that the terrine is easy to cut. Using a sharp carving knife, cut the terrine into 8 slices, then remove the cling film. Heat a large non-stick frying pan over a medium heat, spray with a little oil and then add the slices of terrine. Season with salt and pepper. Cook for about 3 minutes on each side until the terrine is golden brown and crisp.

To serve, dress the rocket leaves in the truffle oil. Serve the hot terrine on a bed of rocket and spoon on a little of the avocado purée. Garnish with parsley.

Champneys rating

SERVES 4

800 g/1 lb 12 oz **skate wings**

1 kg/2¼ lb **potatoes**, peeled and cut into 2 cm/¾ inch dice

salt and **pepper**

1 over-ripe **avocado**

juice of 1 **lemon**

pinch of **chilli powder**

cooking oil in a spray can

1 bunch **rocket**

1 teaspoon **truffle oil**

flat-leaf **parsley**, to garnish

roasted fillets of cod
with mango and tomato salsa

First make the salsa: place the mango, onion and tomatoes in a bowl, add the remaining ingredients, mix and refrigerate.

Heat the oven to 200°C/400°F/gas 6 and put a baking sheet in the oven to heat up.

Trim the asparagus into 5 cm/2 inch pieces, and, if necessary, trim the thick part of the stem with a potato peeler. Steam the asparagus for 5 minutes.

Heat the olive oil in a non-stick frying pan. Add the fish fillets, flesh side down, and fry for 2 minutes. Place the fish skin side down on the preheated baking sheet, add the asparagus and roast in the hot oven for 7 minutes.

Using the same frying pan, stir-fry the spinach or chard until tender. Drain and season to taste with salt and pepper. Place the spinach in the centre of 4 serving plates, pile the asparagus on top and lastly the crisp-skinned fish. Serve with a little of the salsa around the outside.

Champneys rating

SERVES 4

2 bunches **asparagus**

2 tablespoons **olive oil**

4 young **cod** fillets (about 140 g/5 oz each), scaled, skin left on, boned

800 g/1 lb 12 oz **baby spinach** or **swiss chard**

salt and freshly ground **black pepper**

mango and tomato salsa

½ **mango**, peeled and finely diced

1 small **red onion**, finely diced

2 ripe **red tomatoes**, skinned, deseeded and diced

2 ripe **yellow tomatoes**, skinned, deseeded and diced

1 **garlic clove**, finely chopped

1 bunch **chives**, chopped

1 tablespoon **sugar**

2 teaspoons **extra virgin olive oil**

1 tablespoon **sherry vinegar**

dash of **sweet chilli sauce**

rabbit with parma ham

and caramelized onions, orange and pearl barley risotto

Separate 2 slices of Parma ham and set aside. Put the remaining 4 slices under a very low grill so the ham gently dries out and becomes crisp. This should take approximately 30 minutes.

In a thick-bottomed frying pan over a low heat, sweat the onions in half the oil, stirring regularly so that the onions caramelize but do not burn; this may take 20–25 minutes. When the onions have caramelized, add the lemon thyme leaves and orange juice and season to taste with salt and pepper. Dice the reserved 2 slices of Parma ham and add to the onions. Leave to cool.

Heat the oven to 230°C/450°F/gas 8. Divide the onion mixture into four and use to stuff the rabbit legs; tie up with string. Heat a roasting tin, add the remaining oil and when the oil is hot, seal the rabbit legs until golden brown on both sides. Then place in the hot oven and roast for 20–25 minutes, turning occasionally.

To make the risotto, put the pearl barley, shallots and bay leaves in a thick-bottomed saucepan over a medium heat. Add the stock a little at a time, bringing to the boil and stirring until the stock has been absorbed each time. The risotto should be cooked until it has a creamy consistency. Finally, stir in the orange zest and juice, parsley and fromage frais. Season to taste with a little salt and black pepper.

If you would like a sauce for the rabbit, remove the rabbit from the roasting tin and set aside. Deglaze the tin with white wine. Add the orange zest and juice and the sugar and bring to the boil over a medium-high heat. Season to taste, then pass through a fine sieve.

Serve the rabbit on a bed of risotto and pour over a little sauce, if using. Serve the crisp Parma ham on top and garnish with parsley.

Champneys rating

SERVES 4

6 large slices of **parma ham**

4 **onions**, sliced

2 teaspoons **grapeseed oil**

4 sprigs **lemon thyme**

juice of 1 **orange**

salt and **pepper**

4 **rabbit legs**, boned

chopped **parsley** to garnish

orange and pearl barley risotto

100 g/3½ oz **pearl barley**

6 **shallots**, finely chopped

2 **bay leaves**

2 litres/3½ pints **chicken stock**

finely grated zest and juice of

 1 **orange**

½ bunch **parsley**, chopped

100 ml/3½ fl oz **fromage frais**

sauce (optional)

3 tablespoons **dry white wine**

grated zest and juice of 1 **orange**

1 teaspoon **sugar**

poached chicken breast
with bread sauce, garlic, parsley and thyme

Heat the oven to 200°C/400°F/gas 6. Peel the outer papery skin from the garlic and roast in the hot oven for 10 minutes. Remove all fat and sinews from the chicken and place the breasts in an ovenproof dish. Put the milk in a saucepan, together with the whole roasted garlic bulb, the onions, bay leaves and cloves. Bring slowly to simmering point and simmer for 5 minutes, then pour over the chicken breasts. Pick half the lemon thyme leaves and add to the chicken. Cover with a lid and place in the oven for 15–20 minutes until the chicken is cooked.

Remove the chicken breasts from the milk and keep warm. Strain the milk into a measuring jug, then divide between two saucepans. Stir the breadcrumbs into one pan and cook over a low heat until the sauce thickens. Stir in the fromage frais, then remove from the heat and keep warm. Season to taste with salt and pepper.

Separate the cloves of garlic and add to the second saucepan of milk. Bring to the boil, then whisk in the dissolved cornflour to thicken to a coating consistency. Add the chopped parsley and lemon zest and cook for 2 minutes. Add a little lemon juice and season to taste. Liquidize and then pass through a fine sieve.

To serve, spoon the bread sauce on to 4 serving plates and place the chicken on top. Drizzle the parsley and garlic sauce around the chicken and finish by sprinkling the remaining lemon thyme over the chicken.

Champneys rating

SERVES 4

1 whole **garlic bulb**

4 organic **chicken breasts**, skinned and boned

500 ml/16 fl oz **semi-skimmed milk**

2 **onions**, finely chopped

4 **bay leaves**

3 **cloves**

1 bunch **lemon thyme**

100 g/3½ oz fresh **breadcrumbs**

4 tablespoons **fromage frais**

salt and **pepper**

1 tablespoon **cornflour** dissolved in a little water

1 bunch **parsley**, finely chopped

grated zest and juice of 2 **lemons**

slow-braised pork fillet with chinese spices
and stir-fried sweet and sour vegetables

Heat the oven to 190°C/375°F/gas 5. Trim all the fat from the pork fillets and lay them in an ovenproof dish with a lid. In a bowl, mix the soy sauce, plum sauce, rice wine, tomato purée, five-spice powder, ground ginger, coriander seeds, caraway seeds and bay leaves. Cook the onions and garlic in a non-stick pan over a low heat until they caramelize. Blend the cooked onion and garlic together with the spice mixture in a liquidizer for 3 minutes. Pour the liquid over the pork, cover with a lid and place in the oven for 2 hours.

To make the sweet and sour sauce, boil the pineapple juice, star anise, ginger, sugar and vinegar over a high heat until it has reduced to a light syrup. Then add the soy sauce and tomato juice and warm gently. Strain the sauce through a fine sieve and keep warm.

Heat a non-stick pan or wok over a high heat. Add the sesame oil, then add the vegetables and stir-fry for 30 seconds. Add 1 tablespoon of the sweet and sour sauce and cook for a further 2–3 minutes, stirring constantly. The vegetables should remain crisp.

To serve, spoon the vegetables on to 4 serving plates and put the pork fillets on top. Drizzle a little sweet and sour sauce and thick soy sauce around the vegetables. Put the chives on the pork and serve at once.

Champneys rating

SERVES 4

4 organic **pork fillets** (140 g/5 oz each)

2 tablespoons each of **light soy sauce**, **plum sauce**, **rice wine**

4 tablespoons **tomato purée**

pinch of **five-spice powder**

2 pinches of **ground ginger**

30 **coriander seeds**, crushed

1 teaspoon **caraway seeds**

4 **bay leaves**, crushed

2 **onions**, sliced

5 **garlic cloves**, sliced

1 tablespoon **thick soy sauce**

1 bunch **chives**, cut into batons

sweet and sour vegetables

100 ml/3½ fl oz **pineapple juice**

3 **star anise**, crushed

1 teaspoon grated **fresh ginger**

1 tablespoon **sugar**

3 tablespoons **vinegar**

1 tablespoon **light soy sauce**

3 tablespoons **tomato juice**

1 teaspoon **sesame oil**

2 small **pak choi**, shredded

1 small **carrot** and 1 small **courgette**, cut into 2 cm/¾ inch matchsticks

1 **red pepper**, in 2 cm/¾ inch dice

25 g/1 oz **beansprouts**

4 **spring onions**, sliced

cauliflower, lentil and spinach dahl
with wholemeal chapati

To make the chapati, mix the flour with the salt and make a well in the centre. Add the oil and just enough cold water to make a soft dough. Knead for 2 minutes until smooth, then divide the mixture into 8. Roll into small balls, then roll out with a rolling pin to 1 mm thick. Cover with a damp cloth and set aside until ready to cook.

Sweat the onions in the vegetable oil over a low heat with the cumin, turmeric, ground coriander, garam masala, curry paste, grated ginger, chopped chilli and garlic for 30 minutes, stirring occasionally so that the mixture does not burn. Meanwhile, put the red lentils and Puy lentils in separate saucepans with cold water to cover, bring to the boil and simmer for 15 minutes or until tender.

Add the tomato purée and the cooked lentils to the onion mixture and cook for 5 minutes. Add the cauliflower and cook for a further 15 minutes. Add the spinach and the fresh coriander. The dahl is now cooked, but if left to go cold and then reheated the flavour will improve.

To cook the chapati, place a non-stick fryng pan over a high heat, add the chapati in batches and cook for 2 minutes on each side, turning once. They should be patched with dark brown and slightly puffed up.

Mix the yoghurt with the saffron and a little salt to taste. Stir the tomatoes into the warmed dahl mixture and season to taste with salt and lemon juice. Serve the dahl with freshly cooked chapati and the saffron yoghurt.

Champneys rating

SERVES 4

4 **onions**, sliced

2 teaspoons **vegetable oil**

1 teaspoon each of **ground cumin, turmeric, ground coriander, garam masala, mild curry paste** and grated **fresh ginger**

1 fresh **red chilli**, finely chopped

6 **garlic cloves**, finely chopped

100 g/3½ oz **red split lentils**

50 g/2 oz **puy lentils**

2 tablespoons **tomato purée**

200 g/7 oz **cauliflower**, cut into florets

200 g/7 oz **young spinach**, washed

1 bunch **coriander**, chopped

2 tablespoons **low-fat greek yoghurt**

pinch of **saffron strands**, soaked in a little **warm water**

salt

3 **tomatoes**, skinned, deseeded and diced

juice of 1 **lemon**

wholemeal chapati

400 g/14 oz **wholemeal flour**

1 teaspoon **salt**

1 teaspoon **vegetable oil**

sweet potato and caramelized onion bake
with tomato chutney

To make the chutney, put the onion in a small saucepan with the port, balsamic vinegar, curry paste and maple syrup and boil to reduce until syrupy. Add the tomatoes and cook for 1 minute.

Heat the oven to 200°/400°F/gas 6. Cut the sweet potatoes lengthways into 5 mm/¼ inch thick slices. Lay the slices on a baking sheet lined with baking parchment and roast for about 15 minutes or until tender. Add the thyme to the baking sheet for the last 3 minutes of cooking time.

While the potatoes are in the oven, cook the sliced onions in a non-stick pan over a low heat until the onions are caramelized. Season to taste with salt and pepper.

Layer the sweet potato with the mozzarella and caramelized onions, seasoning each layer and finishing with mozzarella, making 4 individual portions. Scatter the roasted thyme leaves over the top and return to the oven for 5 minutes until the mozzarella melts.

To serve, reheat the chutney over a low heat. Serve the layered sweet potato bakes on a bed of tomato chutney.

Champneys rating

SERVES 4

2 **sweet potatoes** (about 800 g/ 1 lb 12 oz in total), peeled

salt and **pepper**

4 large **onions**, sliced

100 g/3½ oz **buffalo mozzarella**, thinly sliced

1 bunch fresh **thyme**

tomato chutney

1 small **onion**, finely chopped

100 ml/3½ fl oz **port**

50 ml/2 fl oz **balsamic vinegar**

1 teaspoon **curry paste**

2 teaspoons **maple syrup**

5 large **tomatoes**, skinned, deseeded and finely diced

duck with ginger and blackcurrants

parsnip and mustard purée

Cut each duck breast diagonally into 3 pieces. Mix the sherry with the blackcurrant jam, ginger, garlic and passata. Liquidize and pour over the duck. Place in the refrigerator for at least 4 hours.

For the parsnip crisps, use a potato peeler to shave the parsnip into thin strips. Place on a baking sheet, spray lightly with oil and then place in a cool oven (130°C/250°F/gas ½) until golden brown and crisp. This will take 2–3 hours, but can be done in advance; leave to cool, then store in an airtight container.

For the parsnip purée, cook the parsnips in salted boiling water for 25 minutes. Drain the parsnips, then place in a food processor with the mustard and fromage frais and blend until smooth. Season to taste with salt and pepper and keep warm.

Meanwhile, heat the oven to 200°C/400°F/gas 6. For the parsnip chips, cut the parsnips into batons. Mix the honey and mustard in a bowl, add the parsnips and toss to coat them in the mixture, then roast on a baking sheet lined with baking parchment or 20 minutes until browned and tender.

Strain the marinade from the duck into a small saucepan, add half the blackcurrants and boil to reduce the liquid by one-third. Pass through a fine sieve and add to the remaining blackcurrants.

Heat a non-stick pan over a high heat and cook the duck for about 2 minutes on each side until cooked pink. Add the blackcurrant sauce and cook for a further minute.

To serve, divide the the parsnip purée between 4 serving plates. Add the honey-roast parsnip chips, then the duck and finish with the parsnip crisps, if using. Spoon a little sauce around the purée.

Champneys rating

SERVES 4

4 **duck breasts** (200 g/7 oz each), skin and fat removed

100 ml/3½ fl oz **dry sherry**

2 tablespoons **blackcurrant jam**

2 teaspoons finely chopped **fresh ginger**

1 **garlic clove**, crushed

3 tablespoons **tomato passata**

2 tablespoons **blackcurrants**

4 sprigs **thyme**, dried out in a cool oven for 10 minutes

parsnip crisps (optional)

1 large **parsnip**

sunflower oil in a spray can

parsnip and mustard purée

500 g/1 lb 2 oz **parsnips**

1 teaspoon **wholegrain mustard**

1 tablespoon **fromage frais**

salt and **pepper**

honey-roast parsnip chips

500 g/1 lb 2 oz **parsnips**

1 teaspoon **clear honey**

1 teaspoon **english mustard**

fillet of beef
with thai green risotto
and shiitake mushrooms

Cut the steaks horizontally into 3 thin medallions, then lightly beat each medallion until it is about 2 mm/⅛ inch thick. Mix the light soy sauce, rice wine, sugar, garlic, coriander, ginger and cornflour together, then brush the mixture over the thin layers of beef and place in the refrigerator for 2 hours.

To make the risotto, dry-sweat the shallots in a thick-bottomed saucepan over a low heat – do not let them colour. Meanwhile, heat the stock. Add the rice to the shallots, together with the lime zest, curry paste and lime leaves; stir well. Add the stock a ladleful at a time, stirring frequently so that the starch in the rice is released. Add the stock gradually; bring to the boil and let the rice absorb the liquid before adding more. This will take 15–20 minutes.

When the rice is swollen and all the stock has been used, remove the lime leaves and stir in the ginger, lime juice, fromage frais and coconut milk. Season to taste with a little salt and then stir in the chopped coriander and basil. Keep warm.

Steam the shiitake mushrooms for 5 minutes. Heat a non-stick pan over a high heat and cook the beef for 1½ minutes on each side. Finish cooking the mushrooms on the pan on which you have cooked the beef.

To serve, layer the beef and mushrooms on top of the risotto. Drizzle with thick soy sauce and garnish with chervil.

Champneys rating

SERVES 4

4 organic **fillet steaks** (about 120 g/ 4 oz each)

2 tablespoons **light soy sauce**

2 tablespoons **shaoxing rice wine**

2 tablespoons **sugar**

3 **garlic cloves**, crushed

3 teaspoons **ground coriander**

1 teaspoon **ground ginger**

1 teaspoon **cornflour**

50 g/2 oz fresh **shiitake mushrooms**

1 tablespoon **thick soy sauce**

4 sprigs **chervil**

thai green risotto

4 **shallots**, chopped

750 ml/1¼ pints **vegetable stock**

100 g/3½ oz **arborio rice**

finely grated zest and juice of 3 **limes**

2 teaspoons **green curry paste**

4 **lime leaves**

½ teaspoon grated **fresh ginger**

3 tablespoons **fromage frais**

2 tablespoons **coconut milk**

salt

1 bunch **coriander**, chopped

1 bunch **basil**, chopped

beans on toast

with melted smoked goats' cheese

To cook the pulses, if using dried, soak in cold water for at least 8 hours, then drain and cover with fresh cold water. Bring to the boil and boil for 2–3 hours; do not add salt as this will make the skins tough and inhibit the beans from cooking all the way through. If using tinned beans, just rinse and set aside.

For the tomato sauce, heat the oven to 220°C/425°F/gas 7. Cut 400 g/14 oz of the tomatoes in half. Squeeze out the seeds, then roast the tomatoes in the oven for 15 minutes. Blanch, peel, deseed and dice the remaining tomatoes and set aside.

In a thick-bottomed saucepan, sweat three-quarters of the chopped onion with the roasted garlic, tomato purée and roasted tomatoes. Add the wine, stock, bay leaves, cumin, paprika, chilli powder and sugar and cook very slowly over a low heat until the mixture has reduced by two-thirds.

Meanwhile, in a separate saucepan, cook the remaining onion in the olive oil over a low heat until the onion caramelizes.

Add the cooked beans to the caramelized onion. Pass the tomato mixture through a sieve and add to the beans. Simmer on a low heat for 20–30 minutes until the beans have absorbed the tomato sauce.

Add the diced tomato and pepper to the beans. Season to taste with a little salt and pepper and spoon on to the toasted bread, making sure that the toast is totally covered with the beans so that the edges do not burn. Lay the goats' cheese on top and place under a very hot grill until golden brown.

Champneys rating

SERVES 4

50 g/2 oz cooked **borlotti beans**

50 g/2 oz cooked **flageolet beans**

50 g/2 oz cooked **haricot beans**

50 g/2 oz cooked **blackeye beans**

50 g/2 oz cooked **kidney beans**

4 thick slices **wholemeal bread**,
   lightly toasted on both sides

90 g/3 oz **smoked** (or unsmoked)
   goats' cheese, cut into 4 slices

tomato sauce

500 g/1 lb 2 oz ripe **tomatoes**

2 small **onions**, chopped

6 **garlic cloves**, roasted then peeled

1 tablespoon **tomato purée**

3 tablespoons **dry white wine**

150 ml/5 fl oz **vegetable stock**

2 **bay leaves**

pinch of **ground cumin**

pinch of **paprika**

pinch of **chilli powder**

2 tablespoons **sugar**

1 tablespoon **olive oil**

1 **red pepper**, roasted, skinned,
   deseeded and diced

salt and **pepper**

braised chicken legs
with bubble and squeak

Heat the oven to 190°C/375°F/gas 5. In a casserole, fry the onions in the olive oil until browned. Add the shallots, carrots, celery, turnips, swede, leeks, garlic and mushrooms and cook until lightly browned. Add the wine and boil until reduced by half, then add the bay leaves, sage, passata, stock and chicken pieces. Cover with a lid, bring to the boil, then place in the oven for 1¼ hours.

To make the bubble and squeak, blanch the cabbage in salted boiling water for 3 minutes, then drain, refresh under cold running water, drain well and dry in a clean tea towel. Mash the potatoes and add the cabbage, parsley, sage and salt and pepper to taste. Divide into 4 pieces, roll in the flour and shape into 5 cm diameter cakes. Heat a non-stick frying pan, add the olive oil and when it is hot add the potato cakes and brown on both sides. Transfer the cakes to the oven to finish cooking for 10−15 minutes until golden brown.

Remove the casserole from the oven and lift the chicken and vegetables out of the cooking liquid; keep warm. Discard the bay leaves and sage. Boil the liquid until it reduces and thickens. Season to taste with salt and pepper and return the vegetables and chicken to the sauce to reheat for 3−4 minutes. Serve the vegetables on 4 plates, with the bubble and squeak and the chicken pieces on top. Pour the sauce over the chicken and garnish with parsley.

Champneys rating

SERVES 4

2 **onions**, sliced

1 teaspoon **olive oil**

4 **shallots**, peeled

2 **carrots**, quartered lengthways

3 sticks **celery**, cut in half

100 g/3½ oz small **turnips**, quartered

100 g/3½ oz **swede** and
    4 small **leeks**, cut into 3 cm/
    1 inch pieces

2 **garlic cloves**, crushed

8 **button mushrooms**

150 ml/5 fl oz **red wine**

2 **bay leaves**, 2 sprigs **sage**

100 ml/3½ fl oz **tomato passata**

500 ml/16 fl oz good **chicken stock**

4 organic **chicken legs**, cut into
    drumsticks and thighs, skin removed

salt and **pepper**

chopped **parsley**, to garnish

bubble and squeak

150 g/5 oz **savoy cabbage**, shredded

4 large **potatoes**, cooked in
    their jackets

1 teaspoon chopped **parsley**

½ teaspoon chopped **sage**

4 tablespoons **wholemeal flour**

1 tablespoon **olive oil**

loin of venison

with garlic mashed potato, mushy peas and morels

Put the venison in a shallow dish. Mix all the ingredients for the marinade together and pour over the venison. Cover with cling film and leave in the refrigerator for 12 hours. Put the marrowfat peas in a bowl, cover with cold water and leave to soak overnight.

The next day, lift the venison out of the marinade using a slotted spoon and set aside. Pour the marinade into a saucepan, add the stock and slowly bring to the boil, skimming off any scum that rises to the surface. Simmer over a moderate heat until reduced by three-quarters. Pass through a fine sieve and add the soaked morels. Cover with cling film until ready to use.

Meanwhile, simmer the marrowfat peas with just enough water to cover for 1½ hours until tender and cooked to a purée. Mix the purée (or canned peas) with the chopped mint and vinegar. Season to taste with salt and pepper. Keep warm.

For the garlic mashed potato, heat the oven to 220°C/425°F/gas 7. Roast the garlic clove in its skin for 15–20 minutes until soft. Boil the potatoes in salted water until soft. Drain and mash the potatoes with the roasted garlic, olive oil spread and fromage frais. Season to taste with salt and pepper. Keep warm.

To cook the venison, heat a non-stick pan (with an ovenproof handle) over a high heat and then seal the meat for 1 minute on each side. Transfer to the oven and roast for 12–15 minutes until tender but still pink in the centre. Meanwhile, reheat the morels in the reduced marinade.

Pile the mashed potato and mushy peas in the centre of 4 plates. Place the venison on top and spoon the morels around the outside.

Champneys rating

SERVES 4

4 organic **venison steaks** (about 100 g/3½ oz each), cut from the loin, all skin, sinews and fat removed

100 g/3½ oz **dried marrowfat peas** (or a 400 g/14 oz tin of mushy peas)

250 ml/8 fl oz **chicken** or **game stock**

15 g/½ oz **dried morels**, soaked in hot water to cover

½ teaspoon finely chopped **mint**

1 teaspoon **white wine vinegar**

salt and **pepper**

marinade

1 tablespoon **honey**

100 ml/3½ fl oz **madeira**

1 tablespoon fresh **thyme leaves**

1 **garlic clove**, sliced

1 teaspoon **sherry vinegar**

15 g/½ oz **dried ceps** (porcini mushroms)

1 **onion**, 1 **leek**, 1 stick **celery** and 2 **carrots**, chopped

garlic mashed potato

1 **garlic clove**

200 g/7 oz **potatoes**, quartered

1 tablespoon **olive oil spread**

1 tablespoon **fromage frais**

braised pheasant

with redcurrants, shallots and apricots on citrus couscous

Heat the oven to 180°C/350°F/gas 4. Chop the pheasant legs above the knuckle joint, remove the skin, then wrap each leg in a rasher of bacon; set aside.

Heat a flameproof casserole dish over a medium heat, add the oil and then the shallots and cook until they are golden brown. Add the halved apricots, thyme, sherry, stock, bay leaves, tomato purée, redcurrants and redcurrant jelly. Put the pheasant legs into the mixture, cover with a lid and cook in the oven for 1¼ hours.

To prepare the couscous, mix the citrus fruit zests with the mustard and the chopped apricots. Boil the citrus juices until reduced by two-thirds, then add to the mustard mixture. Mix with the soaked couscous and season to taste with a little salt and pepper.

When the pheasant is cooked, remove from the casserole dish and keep warm. Put the casserole dish over a high heat and boil until the cooking liquid has reduced and thickened. Season to taste.

Serve the couscous in the centre of 4 plates, with the pheasant on top. Remove the thyme and bay leaves from the sauce and pour over the pheasant. Garnish with fresh thyme sprigs.

Champneys rating

SERVES 4

4 **pheasant legs**

4 rashers of **smoked back bacon**, fat removed

1 teaspoon **grapeseed oil**

12 **shallots**, peeled and halved

8 **dried apricots**, halved

4 sprigs **thyme**, plus extra to serve

100 ml/3½ fl oz **medium sherry**

150 ml/5 fl oz **chicken stock**

4 **bay leaves**

1 tablespoon **tomato purée**

120 g/4 oz **redcurrants**

1 tablespoon **redcurrant jelly**

citrus couscous

finely grated zest and juice of 1 **orange**, 1 **lemon** and 1 **lime**

1 teaspoon **dijon mustard with tarragon**

4 **dried apricots**, finely chopped

120 g/4 oz **couscous**, soaked in boiling water for 20–30 minutes

salt and **pepper**

szechwan orange chicken

with hoisin roasted beetroot and spring greens

Cut the chicken breasts in half diagonally and score with a sharp knife on both sides so that the marinade can infuse into the chicken. Mix all the ingredients for the marinade together and rub into the chicken. Place in the refrigerator for at least 4 hours.

To make the sauce, liquidize all the ingredients until smooth. If the sauce is too thick, add a little milk. Pass the mixture through a fine sieve and set aside.

Heat the oven to 220°/425°F/gas 7. Heat a non-stick frying pan (with an ovenproof handle) over a high heat, add the grapeseed oil and sauté the beetroot until golden brown. Push the beetroot to the side of the pan and lightly brown the chicken breasts for about 1 minute on each side. Drizzle the honey and hoisin sauce over the beetroot and then place the pan in the oven for 10 minutes or until the chicken is cooked through.

Meanwhile, cook the spring greens in a wok with a little boiling water and the light soy sauce until tender, about 4 minutes. Drain.

Serve the chicken on top of the greens, with the roasted beetroot. Serve the sauce on the side, sprinkled with a few drops of dark soy sauce.

Champneys rating

SERVES 4

4 organic **chicken breasts**,
   skinned and boned

1 tablespoon **grapeseed oil**

140 g/5 oz **baby beetroot**, cut in half

1 tablespoon **clear honey**

1 teaspoon **hoisin sauce**

140 g/5 oz **spring greens**

1 tablespoon **light soy sauce**

1 tablespoon **dark soy sauce**

marinade

1 tablespoon **szechwan**
   peppercorns, crushed

1 tablespoon **garam masala**

1 teaspoon each of **sesame oil**,
   wasabi paste, **ground ginger**
   and **coriander seeds**, crushed

grated zest and juice of 1 **orange**

2 tablespoons **sake**

1 tablespoon **clear honey**

sauce

1 tablespoon **hoisin sauce**

1 tablespoon grated **fresh ginger**

grated zest and juice of 1 **orange**

1 tablespoon chopped fresh **coriander**

25 g/1 oz **soft tofu**

1–2 tablespoons **milk** (optional)

desserts

When you're looking for a positively healthy pudding, choose fruit. Better still, choose one of these inspired ideas for low-fat desserts that look and taste sensational. And for a change, try Champneys' health-conscious twists on two old favourites, chocolate mousse and trifle.

exotic fruits baked in parchment

with lemon grass and vanilla

Heat the oven to 190°C/375°F/gas 5. In a stainless steel saucepan, boil the strips of lemon peel with the lemon juice, the lemon grass, peppercorns and sugar until they begin to caramelize.

Cut four 30 cm/12 inch squares of baking parchment, good-quality greaseproof paper or aluminium foil; fold diagonally to form triangles. Open each triangle up and pour on a little of the lemon syrup, then arrange the fruits on top, being careful not to pierce the paper and making sure that the fruit covers only the centre one-third of each triangle. Spoon on the passion fruit flesh and add half a vanilla pod. Carefully seal the envelopes, folding the paper over three times to make an airtight seal. Place on a baking sheet and bake for 10–15 minutes until the envelopes have filled with steam.

Mix the fromage frais with the seeds from the vanilla pod and the honey. Serve the fruit-filled envelopes on napkin-lined plates; the envelopes are opened at the table so that diners can enjoy the wonderful aromas released when the bags are opened. Serve the fromage frais separately.

Champneys rating

SERVES 4

2 **lemons**, peeled with a potato peeler, juiced

6 **lemon grass** stalks, split in half, then quartered

8 **pink peppercorns**, crushed

25 g/1 oz **sugar**

2 **kiwi fruit**, peeled and sliced

8 **strawberries**, halved

4 **lychees**, peeled, stones removed

2 **guava**, peeled, cut in half

1 **starfruit**, sliced into 4

2 **nectarines**, stones removed and cut into thick slices

2 **passion fruit**, flesh removed with a teaspoon

2 **vanilla pods**, cut in half lengthways, seeds scraped out and reserved

3 tablespoons **fromage frais**

1 teaspoon **honey**

iced pineapple and aniseed mousse

with grilled pineapple and pepper strawberries

In a thick-bottomed saucepan, boil 100 g/3½ oz of the sugar with 1 tablespoon water, the star anise and the cubed pineapple over a medium heat. Stir occasionally until the pineapple is soft. Liquidize in a food processor until smooth and then pass through a fine sieve into a large bowl. Stir in the lemon zest, fromage frais and yoghurt. Then, either put the mixture into an ice-cream machine and churn until nearly set or put the bowl into the freezer and whisk every 30 minutes until slushy – approximately 2–3 hours.

Meanwhile, heat the oven to 200°C/400°F/gas 6. Cut the baby pineapple into 8 slices: 4 about 5 mm/¼ inch thick and 4 very thin. Peel the thicker slices, place on a baking sheet and roast for 15 minutes. Put the roasted pineapple in the base of 4 individual gateau rings. Brush the very thin slices with honey on both sides. Place on a baking sheet lined with baking parchment and dry out in a very cool oven (100°C/200°F/gas ¼) for 3 hours until crisp.

When the pineapple-yoghurt mixture is nearly frozen, bring the remaining sugar to the boil with 1 teaspoon water over a high heat and boil until it forms a light golden caramel. Whisk the egg whites until soft peaks form, then whisk in the caramel. Fold the egg whites into the pineapple mixture and then pour into the gateau rings. Level the tops and put in the freezer for 2 hours.

Put the peppercorns in a saucepan with 1 teaspoon sugar and the orange juice and zest and simmer for 3–4 minutes, then stir in the sliced strawberries. Remove from the heat.

To serve, cut around the gateau rings with a sharp, hot knife and place the mousse on cold serving plates. Put the crisp pineapple slices on top and finish with the peppered strawberries.

Champneys rating

SERVES 4

120 g/4 oz **sugar**

10 **star anise**

1 small **pineapple**, skin removed,
    cut into 1 cm/½ inch cubes

finely grated zest of 2 **lemons**

50 ml/2 fl oz **fromage frais**

50 ml/2 fl oz **low-fat greek yoghurt**

1 baby **pineapple**, cored

1 tablespoon **clear honey**

2 **egg whites**

1 teaspoon **pink peppercorns**,
    crushed

grated zest and juice of 1 **orange**

90 g/3 oz **strawberries**, thinly sliced

buttermilk pancakes
with roasted bananas, blueberries and apricots

To make the pancake batter, lightly whisk the buttermilk with the egg, then add the sugar. Sift the flour and baking powder together and then whisk into the buttermilk mixture. With a potato peeler, cut thin strips of zest from half the orange and all the lemon; set aside. Finely grate the other half of the orange and whisk into the pancake mixture. Place in the refrigerator for 20 minutes.

Put the strips of orange and lemon zest in a stainless steel saucepan with the juices. Add the cinnamon stick, vanilla pods, bay leaves, apricots and 4 tablespoons water. Place on a low heat and simmer until reduced to a thin syrup.

Heat the oven to 230°C/450°F/gas 8. Cut the bananas in half and then into quarters and place on a baking sheet lined with greaseproof paper. Sprinkle with the icing sugar and put into the oven for 10 minutes until golden brown.

To cook the pancakes, heat a non-stick frying pan on a high heat. Spray with a little oil and pour a small amount of the batter into the centre of the pan; immediately tilt the pan to distribute the mixture evenly. Cook for about 1 minute, then turn over, using a spatula, and cook the other side for 45 seconds. Turn out on to a warm plate and keep warm while you make 7 more pancakes.

Mix the blueberries into the spiced apricot syrup. To serve, lay a piece of banana on each pancake, then spoon on a little of the apricot and blueberry mixture and fold over. Serve with a spoonful of yoghurt.

Champneys rating

SERVES 4

350 ml/12 fl oz **buttermilk**

1 **egg**

25 g/1 oz **caster sugar**

120 g/4 oz **wholemeal flour**

pinch of **baking powder**

1 **orange**

1 **lemon**

1 **cinnamon stick**

2 **vanilla pods**, split

4 **bay leaves**

4 **dried apricots**, quartered

2 small **bananas**

1 teaspoon **icing sugar**

sunflower oil in a spray can

140 g/5 oz **blueberries**

4 tablespoons **low-fat greek yoghurt**

exotic fruit salad

with mango and lemon grass sorbet

First make the sorbet: boil the sugar with the lime juice and lemon grass for 10 minutes. Liquidize the sugar syrup with the mangoes and the lime zest, then pass through a fine sieve. Churn the mixture in an ice-cream machine until frozen.

Meanwhile, for the raspberry syrup, put the raspberries in a small saucepan with the caster sugar and boil over a high heat until they caramelize. Pass through a very fine sieve and cover with cling film to prevent a skin from forming.

Use a selection of fruits – it doesn't matter if you don't have all those listed – and mix them in a large bowl. Split the vanilla pods and scrape the seeds into the fruit salad. Pile the fruit salad on to cold serving dishes, add a scoop of mango sorbet and drizzle a little of the raspberry syrup over the top. Serve at once.

Champneys rating
●●●

SERVES 4

1 **starfruit**, diced

1 small **papaya** (paw paw), peeled and diced

2 **guavas**, peeled and diced

1 **kiwi**, peeled and diced

4 **lychees**, peeled and diced

4 **strawberries**, sliced

25 g/1 oz **blueberries**

25 g/1 oz **redcurrants**

2 **vanilla** pods

mango and lemon grass sorbet

50 g/2 oz **sugar**

grated zest and juice of 2 **limes**

6 large **lemon grass** stalks, finely chopped

2 over-ripe **mangoes**, peeled

raspberry syrup

50 g/2 oz **raspberries**

25 g/1 oz **caster sugar**

iced apricot mousse
with pistachios and warm plum compote

Simmer the apricots in boiling water for 20 minutes, then liquidize with a hand-held blender. Remove 4 tablespoons of the mixture and put into a saucepan with half the orange juice and all the zest and cook over a low heat for 4 minutes until thick, then pass through a fine sieve and leave to cool.

Mix the remaining apricot mixture with the fromage frais, yoghurt and crème fraîche. Split the vanilla pod and scrape the seeds into the apricot mixture. Whisk the egg whites until soft peaks form, then fold into the apricot mixture with a metal spoon, pour into 4 individual gateau rings on a baking sheet and put into the freezer for 4 hours.

To make the plum compote, boil the plums, ginger, ginger syrup, brandy, the remaining orange juice and 4 tablespoons water over a low heat for 10 minutes until the plums are soft but still keeping their shape. Mix the arrowroot with a little water and stir into the boiling plum mixture to thicken slightly.

Slide a warm knife around the gateau rings to remove the mousses. Roll the mousses in chopped pistachios, then place on 4 serving plates. Spoon the apricot and orange sauce over the mousse and serve the warm plums around the outside.

Champneys rating

SERVES 4

200 g/7 oz **dried apricots**

grated zest and juice of 1 **orange**

2 tablespoons **fromage frais**

2 tablespoons **thick low-fat yoghurt**

2 tablespoons **low-fat crème fraîche**

1 **vanilla pod**

2 **egg whites**

50 g/2 oz **pistachio nuts**, blanched, peeled and finely chopped

plum compote

12 **plums**, cut in half, stones removed

2 slices of **stem ginger** preserved in syrup, diced, plus 2 tablespoons of the **ginger syrup**

½ teaspoon **ground ginger**

2 tablespoons **brandy**

½ teaspoon **arrowroot**

iced prune and almond terrine
with blackcurrant and orange sauce

Soak the prunes in the amaretto, preferably overnight. The terrine must be made on the day that you intend to eat it, as if it is frozen too far in advance it will set too hard.

Line a 1 litre/1¾ pint terrine or loaf tin with greaseproof paper. In a thick-bottomed saucepan, boil the orange juice with the sugar until caramelized. Add the almonds and remove from the heat. Stir the almonds to coat them in the caramel, then leave to cool.

Put the soaked prunes and amaretto, almonds, fromage frais and half the orange zest in a food processor. Split the vanilla pods and scrape the seeds into the processor. Blend until smooth and pour into a large bowl. Whisk the egg whites until soft peaks form, then fold into the prune mixture with a metal spoon. Spoon the mixture into the lined terrine and place in the freezer. It will take at least 4 hours to freeze.

To make the sauce, boil half the blackcurrants with the remaining orange zest. Add the caster sugar and cook for 3−4 minutes until the fruit has collapsed to a purée. Pass the mixture through a fine sieve, add to the remaining blackcurrants and leave to cool.

To serve, dip the base of the terrine into warm water, taking care not to let water get into the terrine, then turn out on to a chopping board. Cut into 2 cm/¾ inch thick slices and slice diagonally. Serve on cold plates. Pour a little of the sauce around the outside and garnish with almonds and candied orange zest.

Champneys rating

SERVES 10

300 g/11 oz **prunes**, stones removed

150 ml/5 fl oz **amaretto liqueur**

grated zest and juice of 4 **oranges**

25 g/1 oz **sugar**

100 g/3½ oz **whole almonds**

600 ml/18 fl oz **low-fat fromage frais**

2 **vanilla pods**

3 **egg whites**

200 g/7 oz **blackcurrants**

25 g/1 oz **caster sugar**

whole almonds and **candied orange zest** (see page 154), to garnish

caramelized marsala pears
with polenta and almond biscuits

First make the biscuits; this can be done a day ahead. Cream the fat and sugar. Add the polenta and ground almonds and then the wholemeal flour. Wrap and leave to rest in the refrigerator for 20 minutes. Heat the oven to 180°C/350°F/gas 4. Roll out the dough to about 3 mm/⅛ inch thick and cut out with a 5 cm/2 inch diameter plain cutter, making 12–14 biscuits. Place on a non-stick baking sheet and bake for 15–20 minutes until golden brown. Cool on a wire rack and store in an airtight container.

For the pears, heat a frying pan over a high heat and add the marsala and sugar. Once they have caramelized, add the pears and cook until lightly coloured. Take care not to overcook the pears; they should be tender but still firm. Strain the pears, return the juices to the pan and boil to reduce by two-thirds. Add the mixed spice and blackberries, cook for 2 minutes and then leave to cool.

Mix the mascarpone, yoghurt and lemon zest. Assemble the dessert with layers of polenta biscuits – 3 per person – mascarpone mixture and pears. Spoon the blackberries and juices around the edge of the plate and serve at once.

Champneys rating

SERVES 4

4 ripe **pears**, peeled and cut into quarters or sixths, depending on their size

100 ml/3½ fl oz **marsala**

25 g/1 oz **sugar**

pinch of **ground mixed spice**

100 g/3½ oz **blackberries**

3 tablespoons **mascarpone**

100 ml/3½ fl oz **low-fat greek yoghurt**

grated zest of 1 **lemon**

polenta and almond biscuits

50 g/2 oz **olive oil spread**

50 g/2 oz **caster sugar**

25 g/1 oz **polenta**

50 g/2 oz **ground almonds**

50 g/2 oz **wholemeal flour**

spiced apple sorbet

with apple crisps and blackberries

First make the apple crisps; this can be done a day ahead. Slice very thinly across the whole apples with a very sharp knife. Pat dry on kitchen paper. Gently warm the lemon juice with the icing sugar until the sugar dissolves. Brush the apple slices with this syrup on both sides. Lay on a baking sheet lined with baking parchment and dry out in a very cool oven for 3 hours until crisp. Store in an airtight container.

In a saucepan, bring to the boil the apple juice with the cinnamon, star anise, cloves, bay leaves, allspice, mixed spice, ginger, orange and lemon zests. Add the sugar and simmer for 5 minutes, then pass through a fine sieve into a large bowl and leave to cool. Take the Cox's apples from the freezer and coarsely grate them into the cold spiced apple juice. Churn in an ice-cream machine or place the bowl in the freezer and whisk every 30 minutes until frozen; this will take about 2 hours.

In a small saucepan, bring the orange juice to the boil with the honey. Boil for 2 minutes, then toss the blackberries in the syrup and leave to cool.

To serve, scoop balls of sorbet and layer with 3 or 4 apple crisps. Spoon the blackberries around the edge and serve with a small spoonful of yoghurt, lightly dusted with mixed spice.

Champneys rating

♥

SERVES 4

2 **cox's apples**, cored and frozen
  overnight

250 ml/8 fl oz **natural cloudy
  apple juice**

3 **cinnamon sticks**

4 **star anise**

4 **cloves**, crushed

4 **bay leaves**

¼ teaspoon **ground allspice**

pinch of **mixed spice**, plus extra
  to dust

3 cm/1 inch piece of **fresh ginger**,
  sliced

zest of 1 **orange**, peeled with a
  potato peeler, juiced

zest of 1 **lemon**, peeled with a
  potato peeler

50 g/2 oz **sugar**

1 teaspoon **honey**

140 g/5 oz **blackberries**

2 tablespoons **thick low-fat yoghurt**

apple crisps

2 large **bramley apples**

juice of 1 **lemon**

2 tablespoons **icing sugar**

cold rhubarb, date and mango crumble

with papaya custard

Heat the oven to 200°C/400°F/gas 6. Put the rhubarb in an ovenproof dish, sprinkle with the icing sugar and roast for 15–20 minutes until cooked. Reduce the oven to 190°C/375°F/gas 5.

Strain the rhubarb over a small saucepan to collect the juice; leave the rhubarb to cool. Carefully split the vanilla pods lengthways and scrape the seeds into the rhubarb juice; reserve the pods. Add the orange juice and half the papaya to the rhubarb juice, place the pan on a high heat and reduce by two-thirds. Liquidize with the crème fraîche, pass through a fine sieve and leave to cool.

To make the crumble mixture, put the oats, flour, sugar, hazelnuts, olive oil spread and orange zest into a food processor and blend to the consistency of breadcrumbs. Sprinkle on to a non-stick baking sheet and cook for about 20 minutes, turning occasionally and breaking up any lumps. Leave to cool. Reduce the oven to its lowest setting.

Carefully cut the vanilla pods lengthways into very thin strips, place on a baking sheet in the cool oven and allow to become dry and crisp.

Mix the cold rhubarb with the dates and mango and push into individual gateau rings or ramekins, leaving 1 cm/½ inch at the top. Fill with the crumble mixture, then – if using gateau rings – transfer to serving plates and turn out. Add the remaining papaya to the custard and serve around the crumble. Decorate with the crisp vanilla pods. This dish can be made a couple of hours in advance and kept in the refrigerator.

Champneys rating

SERVES 4

6 sticks **rhubarb**, chopped

1 tablespoon **icing sugar**

2 **vanilla pods**

grated zest of 1 **orange**, juice of
   3 **oranges**

1 small **papaya**, peeled, deseeded
   and diced

1 tablespoon **low-fat crème fraîche**

2 tablespoons **rolled oats**

1 tablespoon **wholemeal flour**

25 g/1 oz **muscovado sugar**

2 teaspoons chopped toasted
   hazelnuts

1 tablespoon **olive oil spread**

2 **Medjool dates**, diced

1 small **mango**, peeled and diced

coffee, raspberry and orange soufflé trifle

You will need 4 ramekins or individual soufflé dishes. Cut 4 strips of greaseproof paper long enough to wrap around the outside of the ramekins and wide enough to reach about 3–4 cm/1–1½ inches above the top of the ramekins. Secure the paper around the ramekins with sellotape.

Divide the raspberries between the ramekins. Warm the juice of both oranges with the zest of 1 orange and half of the soaked gelatine. When the gelatine has dissolved, pour over the raspberries and put into the refrigerator to set.

To make the custard, bring the milk to the boil with the sugar and vanilla pod, then whisk in the dissolved cornflour until very thick. Reduce the heat, whisk in the egg yolks and cook for 2–3 minutes, stirring continuously, then leave to cool.

Break the sponge fingers on top of the orange jelly, then pour the cold custard on top. Mix the yoghurt with the remaining orange zest and spoon on top of the custard. The ramekins should now be four-fifths full.

Warm the fromage frais to blood temperature, stir in the kahlua with the remaining gelatine and warm to dissolve. Whisk in the icing sugar. Whisk the egg whites until soft peaks form and fold into the fromage frais mixture with a metal spoon. Spoon into the ramekins to 3 cm/1 inch up the greaseproof paper, then return to the refrigerator to set.

To serve, sprinkle with cocoa powder and carefully remove the greaseproof paper. Serve with more fresh raspberries.

Champneys rating

SERVES 4

90 g/3 oz **raspberries**, plus extra to serve

grated zest and juice of 2 **oranges**

2 teaspoons **gelatine powder**, soaked in water

200 ml/7 fl oz **skimmed milk**

2 tablespoons **muscovado sugar**

1 **vanilla pod**, split

2 tablespoons **cornflour** dissolved in a little water

2 **eggs**, separated

4 **sponge fingers** (Italian savoiardi biscuits)

4 tablespoons **low-fat greek yoghurt**

6 tablespoons **fromage frais**

5 tablespoons **kahlua** (coffee liqueur)

25 g/1 oz **icing sugar**

1 tablespoon **cocoa powder**

lemon and pink grapefruit mousse

with orange biscuits

First make the biscuits; this can be done a day ahead. Cream the fat and sugar with the orange zest and honey, beat in the egg white, then gradually beat in the flour. Leave in the refrigerator for 20 minutes. Heat the oven to 190°C/375°F/gas 5. Spoon the mixture into a large piping bag with a plain 1 cm/½ inch nozzle and pipe strips about 12 cm/5 inches long on to a non-stick baking sheet; this recipe will make about 15 biscuits. Bake for 6 minutes until golden brown. Remove the cooked biscuits using a palette knife and curl over a rolling pin. Leave to set slightly, then remove and cool completely on a wire rack. Store in an airtight container.

To make the mousse, squeeze the grapefruit skin and membranes over a large bowl to extract all the juice. Add the lemon juice, sugar and whole eggs, then whisk over a saucepan of gently simmering water for 10 minutes until the mixture is pale, fluffy and thickened. Take 1 tablespoon of the mixture out and mix with 1 tablespoon of the crème fraîche; reserve for garnish. Whisk the gelatine into the egg mixture, then whisk in the fromage frais and crème fraîche. Whisk the egg whites until stiff and fold into the mousse with a metal spoon. Fold in the chopped grapefruit, then spoon into 4 individual gateau rings on a baking sheet and place in the refrigerator; the mousse will take about 1½ hours to set.

To serve, cut around the gateau rings with a small sharp knife. Serve with 2 orange biscuits and a little of the reserved crème fraîche mixture. Decorate with a few blueberries.

Champneys rating

SERVES 4

1 small **pink grapefruit**, zest peeled with a potato peeler, fruit segmented and finely chopped

juice of 2 **lemons**

50 g/2 oz **caster sugar**

2 **eggs**, plus 2 **egg whites**

100 g/3½ oz **low-fat crème fraîche**

1 **gelatine leaf**, softened in warm water

200 g/7 oz **fromage frais**

a few **blueberries**, to serve

orange biscuits

40 g/1½ oz **olive oil spread**

50 g/2 oz **caster sugar**

grated zest of 1 **orange**

1 tablespoon **clear honey**

1 small **egg white**

90 g/3 oz **flour**

passion fruit yoghurt mousse
with melon sushi and lychees

Begin the day before you want to serve this, by putting the yoghurt into a muslin-lined sieve over a large bowl; leave to strain overnight.

Using a teaspoon, scoop out the pulp and seeds of 10 of the passion fruit and set aside. Bring the milk to the boil with the vanilla pods and 100 g/3½ oz of the sugar. Whisk in the arrowroot solution to thicken the mixture, then stir in the passion fruit pulp and seeds. Stir in the gelatine, cover with cling film and leave to cool slightly.

Put the remaining sugar in a small saucepan with the orange zest and cover with a little water; boil until it forms a light caramel. Whisk the egg whites until soft peaks form, then whisk in the caramel. Strain the milk and passion fruit mixture through a fine sieve and stir into the strained yoghurt, then fold in the egg white mixture using a metal spoon. Pour into a 1 litre/1¾ pint terrine and put into the refrigerator to set; this will take about 2 hours.

Slice the cantaloupe melon very thinly (about 1 mm thick) and cut into pieces measuring 2 x 5 cm/¾ x 2 inches. Cut the watermelon into thick matchsticks, 5 cm/2 inches long. Roll 5 pieces of watermelon inside each piece of cantaloupe; you will need 3 rolls per serving.

To serve, dip the terrine dish into a sink of hot water, being careful not to let the water get into the yoghurt mousse; leave for 30 seconds, then turn out on to a chopping board. Return to the refrigerator for 15 minutes, then cut into 2 cm/¾ inch thick slices. Place on serving plates and add a few lychee halves and 3 melon rolls. Spoon a little of the remaining passion fruit pulp over the top.

Champneys rating

 ♥

SERVES 8

500 ml/16 fl oz **low-fat yoghurt**

12 **passion fruit**

300 ml/10 fl oz **skimmed milk**

2 **vanilla pods**, split

140 g/5 oz **caster sugar**

2 teaspoons **arrowroot**, dissolved
   in 1 tablespoon water

2 teaspoons **gelatine powder**,
   melted in a little warm water

grated zest of 1 **orange**

3 **egg whites**

300 g/11 oz **cantaloupe melon**

140 g/5 oz **watermelon**

12–16 **lychees**, peeled, halved
   and stoned

chilled rice pudding with roasted peaches

cinnamon and honey ice cream

Heat the oven to 190°C/375°F/gas 5. Put the rice, bay leaves, sugar and milk into a non-stick roasting tin and cook for about 2½ hours, stirring after 45 minutes. When the rice is tender, leave to cool.

To make the ice cream, warm the milk with the vanilla pods, cinnamon sticks and mace over a low heat for 15 minutes. Whisk the egg yolks with the honey, add to the milk and stir over a low heat for 8–10 minutes until the custard thickens and coats the back of a wooden spoon. Remove the vanilla pods and cinnamon sticks; rinse the cinnamon sticks in cold water and reserve for a garnish. Stir in the crème fraîche, then pour into an ice-cream machine and churn until ready. Alternatively, put the mixture into a large bowl in the freezer and whisk every 15–20 minutes until set; this will take 3–4 hours.

Heat the oven to 230°C/450°F/gas 8. Blanch the peaches in boiling water for 2 minutes, then refresh in ice-cold water, cut in half and remove the stones. Place the peaches on a baking sheet lined with greaseproof paper and roast for 15 minutes.

To serve, gently warm the raspberry jam. Spoon the cold rice pudding on to 4 serving plates and drizzle the jam over the pudding. Serve the ice cream and warm roasted peaches on top.

Champneys rating

SERVES 4

50 g/2 oz **short-grain pudding rice**

2 **bay leaves**

50 g/2 oz **sugar**

1 litre/1¾ pints **semi-skimmed milk**

4 small **peaches**

2 teaspoons **high fruit raspberry jam**, sieved

cinnamon and honey ice cream

200 ml/7 fl oz **semi-skimmed milk**

2 **vanilla pods**, split

4 **cinnamon sticks**, broken

pinch of **ground mace**

2 **egg yolks**

5 tablespoons **clear honey**

3 tablespoons **low-fat crème fraîche**

champneys chocolate and cointreau mousse

Put the milk and vanilla pods into a saucepan and bring to the boil over a low heat. Add the Cointreau, cocoa and one-third of the sugar. Whisk in the dissolved cornflour to thicken, bring back to the boil and simmer for 2 minutes. Pour through a fine sieve and stir in the fromage frais. Cover with cling film and leave to cool to room temperature.

Whisk the melted gelatine into the cocoa mixture; both mixtures should be at room temperature so that the gelatine does not set in a lump.

Put another one-third of the sugar into a small saucepan with 1 tablespoon water, bring to the boil over a low heat and boil until it starts to turn golden brown. Meanwhile, whisk the egg whites until soft peaks form, then whisk in the hot caramel. Gently fold the egg white mixture into the cocoa mixture with a metal spoon, being careful not to knock the air out. Fold in the grated chocolate. Spoon the mixture either into individual gateau rings or into ramekins. Smooth the tops with a spatula and place in the refrigerator for 45 minutes.

Put the remaining sugar into a small saucepan with the orange juice and heat gently until the sugar dissolves. Then add the strips of zest and cook for 4 minutes until candied.

To serve, cut around the gateau rings with a sharp, hot knife and place the mousse on cold serving plates. Top with a small pile of candied orange zest and dust with cocoa powder. If using ramekins, serve on a plate and decorate with fresh flowers.

Champneys rating

♥   ●●

SERVES 4

300 ml/10 fl oz **semi-skimmed milk**

3 **vanilla pods**, split

4 tablespoons **cointreau**

2 tablespoons **cocoa powder**, plus extra to serve

4 tablespoons **caster sugar**

2 tablespoons **cornflour** dissolved in a little water

25 g/1 oz **fromage frais**

1 teaspoon **gelatine powder**, melted in a little warm water

3 **egg whites**

25 g/1 oz good-quality **dark chocolate** (70% cocoa solids), grated

2 **oranges**, zest peeled with a potato peeler and cut into fine strips, juiced

pear and ginger mousse
with melon granita

Peel and core the pears and use the back of a fork or a liquidizer to mash them until smooth. Add the grated lime zest and then pass the mixture through a sieve into a small saucepan. Add the ginger and the fromage frais, then split the vanilla pod and scrape the seeds into the pan. Gently warm the mixture to blood temperature (you should be able to stick your finger in without burning yourself). Add the soaked gelatine and stir until dissolved. Whisk the egg whites until soft peaks form. Fold the egg whites into the pear mixture and pour into 4 large ramekins. Place in the refrigerator; it will take 1–2 hours to set.

Mash the Ogen melon together with the lime juice and pass the mixture through a sieve into a bowl. Dice the cantaloupe melon and half of the watermelon and add to the Ogen melon purée. Place in the freezer for 2–3 hours, whisking every 20 minutes, so that tiny ice crystals are formed.

Use a melon baller or teaspoon to make melon balls from the remaining watermelon and set aside.

When the pear mousse has set, quickly dip the ramekins into a pan of boiling water and then turn the mousses out on to a pool of the lightly frozen melon mixture. Serve the melon balls on top of the mousse.

Champneys rating

SERVES 4

4 over-ripe **pears**

grated zest and juice of 1 **lime**

2 pieces of **stem ginger** preserved in syrup, finely diced

3 tablespoons **fromage frais**

1 **vanilla pod**

2 **gelatine leaves**, soaked in cold water for 4–5 minutes

2 **egg whites**

1 over-ripe **ogen melon** and 1 small **cantaloupe melon** (or any orange-fleshed melons)

½ small **watermelon**

index

acknowledgements

I would particularly like to thank Lord Thurso and Gillie Turner at Champneys for all their support and encouragement. I would also like to thank Dr Asma Omer for her contribution. Other friends and members of Champneys staff who have provided invaluable help in testing and preparing the recipes for this book include Katy Evers, Nick Heywood, Jon Dunn, Jon Ingram, Jon Boy Waugh, Diana Davies, Carole Ward and Phil Madley. I would also like to thank Philip Webb and his assistant Sarah Cuttle for the great photographs.